The Secret Stitch
A Crochet Companion

by Laurinda Reddig

9 Accessories Inspired by the
Historical Fiber Fiction of C. Jane Reid
Featuring Hand Dyed Yarns and Natural Fibers

For
My Grandmother Diana Smith in her 90th year,
one of the most creative women I know.

Photography: Guy Holtzman (models) and ReCrochetions Designs (tutorials)
Technical Editing: Amy Daraghy, Copy Editing: Carissa Reid
Design and Layout: ReCrochetions Press
Models: Lana Aburto, Aurora Holtzman, Robyn Lowy, and Hollie Stutzman
Quotes from The Secret Stitch by C. Jane Reid

The Secret Stitch: A Crochet Companion
Copyright © 2016 Laurinda Reddig
ReCrochetions Designs

ISBN: 0692678018

ISBN-13: 978-0692678015

CONTENTS

INTRODUCTION

Inspiration for my designs comes from everything I see, and even the things I read. From the time I started designing crochet I found myself reading all of the yarn fiction I could find. There are quite a few knit fiction series out there, but very little crochet fiction. So, I challenged my good friend and neighbor, who happened to be a writer, to remedy that.

A few months later, C. Jane Reid started describing to me her idea for a crochet fiction story with a supernatural twist. When she encouraged me to start a crochet kit club, I suggested that she could write short stories or vignettes to go with each kit that might tie in with the novel she planned to write, perhaps telling the history leading up to the present day character she had dreamed up for her crochet fiction story.

We spent an afternoon brainstorming ideas for stories, which led to design ideas for the first three Ficstitches Yarns Kit Clubs, each with a separate short story. But C. Jane Reid is not a short story writer. About halfway through writing the first story, she was fretting over how to tell Ailee's tale without writing an entire novel. So I told her, "Then write a novel!". And so *The Secret Stitch* came to be.

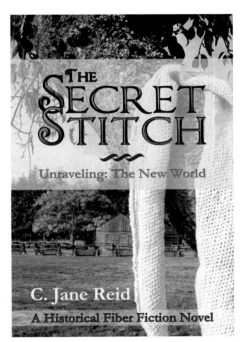

Each day as we walked our young ones to preschool together, we would talk about the story, how the characters were developing, and how the design ideas I already had could be worked in. As she completed sections of the story, she allowed me to read them. Every time she mentioned wool or fiber, I would ponder how I could turn that mention into a crochet design, taking inspiration from the colonial period of her story and adding a modern twist.

Before she was even done writing the novel, I had come up with the collection of designs in these pages. I knew that *A Crochet Companion* was a must to accompany the first in a brand new Historical Crochet Fiction series. Over the next few years, the stories in the *Unraveling Series* will lead up to that first story idea she told me about, with a modern day crocheter learning the history of *The Secret Stitch…*

AILEE'S WEDDING SHAWL

Mrs. Vance held up the shawl. It was a triangle of finely woven ivory linen with cheyne lace in pale thread worked around the edges and three large lace flowers attached at the mid-points. Mrs. Vance gave me a long look. Wordlessly, she folded the shawl and put it back in the bag...

What had Mrs. Vance thought of the shawl? It was a useless thing, I knew. All lace and frail linen, meant for show and splendor. I'd been so proud of myself, hiding a bit of culture from my old life to carry into my new, a piece of my old identity to remind myself that once I'd been well-to-do and admired.

A single skein of fingering weight yarn captures the spirit of Ailee's elegant shawl with a modern interpretation of the treasure she has hidden in her bag as she voyages to a new world. Meant for show and splendor, this lacy shawl with its three delicate Irish Roses will add sophistication to any outfit.

Difficulty
Intermediate

Finished Size
55"(140cm) wingspan,
26"(66cm) long at center

Yarn Used
Approx. 400yds(366m) fingering weight yarn

Yarn used for sample: Black Trillium Lilt Sock, 85% superwash merino/15% mulberry silk (100g/3.5oz, 405yds/370m), 1 hank in Iced Teal

Notions
- Size I/5.5mm crochet hook or hook to get gauge
- Scissors
- Stitch Markers
- Tapestry Needle

Gauge
Before blocking:
15 sts by 9 rows in dc = 4"(10cm);
Small Rose = 2 ¾"(7cm) diameter

PATTERN NOTES

- Shawl is worked from the Large Rose out from center back, joining Small Roses as you go.
- When joining Small Roses to shawl, continue working 'ch 5, sc' loops, inserting the hook through both the normal loop and loop on back of Small Rose before first yarn over of the single crochet, where indicated in the pattern.
- If you have extra, or not enough yarn, you can add or subtract 2 to 4 repeating rows after Small Roses are joined.

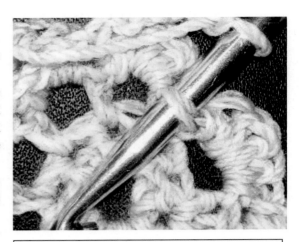

Back of work showing how to insert hook behind petals, through both loops of single crochet two rounds below.

SPECIAL STITCHES

Double crochet 4 together (dc4tog): *Yo, insert hook into next st, yo, pull up a loop, yo, pull through 2 loops; Repeat from * 3 more times, yo, pull through all 5 loops on hook.

Four Double Crochet Cluster (4dcCL): Yo, insert hook in indicated st or sp, yo, pull up a lp, yo, pull through 2 lps on hook, [yo, insert hook in same st or sp, yo, pull up a lp, yo, pull through 2 lps] 3 times, yo, pull through all 5 lps on hook.

SHAWL PATTERN

Small Irish Rose (make 2)
Ch 4, join with sl st to form a ring. Work Rose in rounds, do not turn.

Rnd 1: Ch 1, 8 sc in ring, join with sl st in first sc.

Rnd 2: Ch 1, sc in first sc, [ch 3, sc in next sc] 7 times, ch 2, join with sl st in first sc. (8 ch-sps)

Rnd 3: Sl st in first ch-sp, ch 1, (sc, 3 hdc, sc) in each ch-sp around, join with sl st in first sc. (8 petals)

Rnd 4: Ch 1, working behind each petal, sc in first sc on Rnd 2, [ch 4, sc in next sc on Rnd 2] 7 times, ch 3, join with sl st in first sc.

Rnd 5: Sl st in first ch-sp, ch 1, (sc, 4 hdc, sc) in each ch-sp around, join with sl st in first sc.

Rnd 6: Ch 1, working behind each petal, sc in first sc on Rnd 4, [ch 3, sc in next sc on Rnd 4]

7 times, ch 2, join with sl st in first sc. Finish off and weave in ends. Set aside to attach on Row 19 of Shawl.

Small Rose Diagram
See Large Shawl Diagram for Stitch Symbol Key
(See page 19 for Tips on Reading Diagrams)

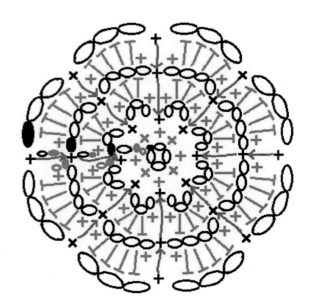

Ailee's Wedding Shawl Stitch Diagram

Stitch Key

+ = Single Crochet (sc)

◯ = Chain (ch)

⬬ = Slip Stitch (sl st)

T = Half Double Crochet (hdc)

₸ = Double Crochet (dc)

Ŧ = Treble Crochet (tr)

⋔ = Double Crochet 4 Together (dc4tog)

↳ = Working behind petals sc into sc of prev rnd

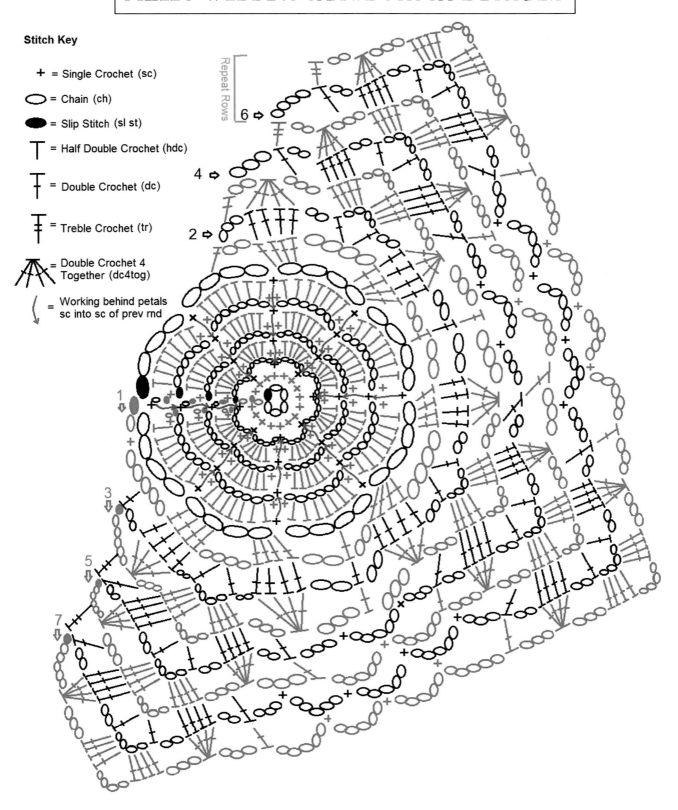

9

Large Irish Rose

Ch 5, join with sl st to form a ring. Work Rose in rounds, do not turn.

Rnd 1: (RS) Ch 1, 16 sc in ring, join with sl st in first sc.

Rnd 2: Ch 1, sc in first sc, [ch 5, sk 1 sc, sc in next sc] 7 times, ch 4, join with sl st in first sc. (8 ch-sps)

Rnd 3: Sl st in first ch-sp, ch 1, (sc, 5 hdc, sc) in each ch-sp around, join with sl st in first sc. (8 petals)

Rnd 4: Ch 1, working behind each petal, sc in first sc on Rnd 2, [ch 6, sc in next sc on Rnd 2] 7 times, ch 5, join with sl st in first sc.

Rnd 5: Sl st in first ch-sp, ch 1, (sc, 6 hdc, sc) in each ch-sp around, join with sl st in first sc.

Rnd 6: Ch 1, working behind each petal, sc in first sc on Rnd 4, [ch 7, sc in next sc on Rnd 4] 7 times, ch 6, join with sl st in first sc.

Rnd 7: Sl st in first ch-sp, ch 1, (sc, 7 hdc, sc) in each ch-sp around, join with sl st in first sc.

Rnd 8: Ch 1, working behind each petal, sc in first sc on Rnd 6, [ch 4, sc in next sc on Rnd 6] 7 times, ch 3, join with sl st in first sc. Do not finish off.

Shawl
Continuing from Large Irish Rose.

Row 1: With RS facing, sl st in first ch-sp, ch 1, sc in same ch-sp, ch 5, [*(4 dc, ch 4, 4 dc) in next ch-sp, ch 2, dc in next ch-sp*, ch 2] 2 times; Rep * to *, turn.

Row 2: (WS) Ch 3, *dc in next 4 dc, ch 2, (dc, ch 4, dc) in next ch-sp, ch 2, dc in next 4 dc, ch 2**, dc in next dc, ch 2; Rep from *; Rep * to **, dc in third ch of last ch-sp, turn.

Row 3: Sl st in first dc, ch 5, *dc4tog, ch 3, sk 1 dc, (4 dc, ch 4, 4 dc) in next ch-sp, ch 3, sk 1 dc, dc4tog**, ch 3, dc in next dc, ch 3; Rep from *; Rep * to **, ch 2, dc in second ch of last ch-sp, turn.

Row 4: Ch 3, *sk next dc4tog, dc in next ch-sp, ch 2, dc in next 4 dc, ch 2, (dc, ch 4, dc) in next ch-sp, ch 2, dc in next 4 dc, ch 2, dc in next ch-sp**, ch 3, sc in next ch-sp, ch 5, sc in next ch-sp, ch 3; Rep from *; Rep * to **, tr in second ch of last ch-sp, turn.

Row 5: Sl st in first dc, ch 5, *dc4tog, ch 3, sk 1 dc, (4 dc, ch 4, 4 dc) in next ch-sp, ch 3, sk 1 dc, dc4tog**, ch 3, dc in next dc, sk ch-3 sp, ch 5, sc in next ch-sp, ch 5, dc in next dc, ch 3; Rep from *; Rep * to **, ch 2, tr in next dc, turn.

Row 6: Ch 4, *sk next dc4tog, dc in next ch-sp, ch 2, dc in next 4 dc, ch 2, (dc, ch 4, dc) in next ch-sp, ch 2, dc in next 4 dc, ch 2, dc in next ch-sp**, ch 3, sc in next ch-sp, (ch 5, sc) in each ch-sp across to next dc4tog, ch 3; Rep from *; Rep * to **, tr in third ch of last ch-sp, turn.

Row 7: Sl st in first dc, ch 5, *dc4tog, ch 3, sk 1 dc, (4 dc, ch 4, 4 dc) in next ch-sp, ch 3, sk 1 dc, dc4tog**, ch 3, dc in next dc, sk ch-3 sp, (ch 5, sc) in each ch-5 sp across, ch 5, sk ch-3 sp, dc in next dc, ch 3; Rep from *; Rep * to

**, ch 2, tr in next dc, turn.

Rows 8-18: Alternate Rows 6 and 7. Ending with Row 6.

Row 19: Sl st in first dc, ch 5, *dc4tog, ch 3, sk 1 dc, (4 dc, ch 4, 4 dc) in next ch-sp, ch 3, sk 1 dc, dc4tog**, ch 3, dc in next dc, sk ch-3 sp, [ch 5, sc in next ch-sp] 7 times, ch 5, sc in next ch-sp and any ch-sp of one Small Rose (Rose joined), [ch 5, sc in next ch-sp] 7 times, ch 5, sk ch-3 sp, dc in next dc, ch 3; Rep from *; Rep * to **, ch 2, tr in next dc, turn.

Row 20: Ch 4, *sk next dc4tog, dc in next ch-sp, ch 2, dc in next 4 dc, ch 2, (dc, ch 4, dc) in next ch-sp, ch 2, dc in next 4 dc, ch 2, dc in next ch-sp**, ch 3, sc in next ch-sp, [ch 5, sc in next ch-sp] 7 times, [ch 5, sc in next ch-sp and next unused ch-sp of Rose] 2 times, [ch 5, sc in next ch-sp] 8 times, ch 3; Rep from *; Rep * to **, tr in third ch of last ch-sp, turn.

Row 21: Sl st in first dc, ch 5, *dc4tog, ch 3, sk 1 dc, (4 dc, ch 4, 4 dc) in next ch-sp, ch 3, sk 1 dc, dc4tog**, ch 3, dc in next dc, sk ch-3 sp, [ch 5, sc in next ch-sp] 7 times, ch 5, sc in next ch-sp and next unused ch-sp of Rose, working behind Rose, ch 5, sc in next ch-sp, ch 5, sc in next ch-sp and next unused ch-sp of Rose, [ch 5, sc in next ch-sp] 7 times, ch 5, sk ch-3 sp, dc in next dc, ch 3; Rep from *; Rep * to **, ch 2, tr in next dc, turn.

Row 22: Ch 4, *sk next dc4tog, dc in next ch-sp, ch 2, dc in next 4 dc, ch 2, (dc, ch 4, dc) in next ch-sp, ch 2, dc in next 4 dc, ch 2, dc in next ch-sp**, ch 3, sc in next ch-sp, [ch 5, sc in next ch-sp] 8 times, [ch 5, sc in next ch-sp and next unused ch-sp of Rose] 2 times, [ch 5, sc in next ch-sp] 9 times, ch 3; Rep from *; Rep * to **, tr in third ch of last ch-sp, turn.

Row 23: Sl st in first dc, ch 5, *dc4tog, ch 3, sk 1 dc, (4 dc, ch 4, 4 dc) in next ch-sp, ch 3, sk 1 dc, dc4tog*, ch 3, dc in next dc, sk ch-3

sp, [ch 5, sc in next ch-sp] 8 times, ch 5, sl st in next ch-sp, work (3dc, ch 4, 3 dc) in next ch-sp and last unused ch-sp of Rose, sl st in next ch-sp, [ch 5, sc in next ch-sp] 8 times, ch 5, sk ch-3 sp, dc in next dc, ch 3; Rep from *; Rep * to **, ch 2, tr in next dc, turn.

Row 24: Ch 4, *sk next dc4tog, dc in next ch-sp, ch 2, dc in next 4 dc, ch 2, (dc, ch 4, dc) in next ch-sp, ch 2, dc in next 4 dc, ch 2, dc in next ch-sp**, ch 3, sc in next ch-sp, [ch 5, sc in next ch-sp] 8 times, ch 5, sl st in next ch-sp, dc in next 3 dc, ch 2, (dc, ch 4, dc) in next ch-sp, ch 2, dc in next 3 dc, sl st in next ch-sp, [ch 5, sc in next ch-sp] 9 times, ch 3; Rep from *; Rep * to **, tr in third ch of last ch-sp, turn.

Row 25: Sl st in first dc, ch 5, *dc4tog, ch 3, sk 1 dc, (4 dc, ch 4, 4 dc) in next ch-sp, ch 3, sk 1 dc, dc4tog**, ch 3, dc in next dc, sk ch-3 sp, [ch 5, sc in next ch-sp] 8 times, ch 5, sl st in next ch-sp, dc3tog over next 3 dc, sl st back into same ch-sp as prev sl st, [ch 5, sc in next ch-sp] 3 times, ch 5, dc3tog over next 3 dc, sl st in next ch-sp, sl st back into gap before dc3tog, [ch 5, sc in next ch-sp] 8 times, ch 5, sk ch-3 sp, dc in next dc, ch 3; Rep from *; Rep * to **, ch 2, tr in next dc, turn.

Rows 26-30: Alternate Rows 6 and 7. Ending with Row 6.

Row 31: Sl st in first dc, ch 5, *dc4tog, ch 3, sk 1 dc, (4 dc, ch 4, 4 dc) in next ch-sp, ch 3, sk 1 dc, dc4tog**, ch 4, sk next dc and 1 ch, sl st in next ch, [ch 1, sk next sc, (4dcCL, ch 4, 4dcCL) in next ch-sp, ch 1, sc in next ch-sp] 13 times, ch 1, (4dcCL, ch 4, 4dcCL) in next ch-sp, ch 1, sk next sc and 2 chs, sl st in next ch, ch 4; Rep from *; Rep * to **, ch 4, sk next dc, sl st in next ch. Do not turn. Do not finish off.

Edging

Begin working in spaces formed by dc, tr, and ch-sps at ends of rows along top edge, including the unused ch-lp on Large Rose. Continue working all the way around.

Rnd 1: Ch 1, [3 sc in next sp, 4 sc in next sp] 14 times, 3 sc in next 2 sps, 2 sc in first open sp of Large Rose, 4 sc in top ch-sp of Rose, 2 sc in next sp of Rose, 3 sc in next sp, [3 sc in next sp, 4 sc in next sp] 15 times, *3 sc in next sp, sk 1 dc, sc in next 3 dc, 6 sc in corner ch-sp, sc in next 3 dc, 3 sc in next sp, 4 sc in next sp**, [2 sc in next sp, 4 sc in next sp, 2 sc in next sp] 14 times, 4 sc in next sp; Rep from *; Rep * to **, join with sl st in first sc, turn.

Rnd 2: Ch 1, sl st loosely in each sc around, join with sl st through center of first sl st. Finish off and weave in all ends.

FINISHING

Wet (or steam) block shawl to relax the stitches and open up the lace. Soak shawl in cool water, roll in a towel, layout flat and pin into a triangle. Chain-loop lace will stretch to form triangle. Use pins to create a gentle curve along the top edge. Place a pin between each set of two 4dcCLs to form points along bottom edge.

Alternative Design Ideas
- Work Flowers in a Different Color than the rest of the shawl so they pop out more.
- Skip the Smaller Flowers and just continue worked the repeated rows.
- Add a second skein for a Larger Shawl, working even more repeated rows before working final edging row.

13

TAVEY'S SATCHEL

"It's a small thing," I lied as the woman tsked over the sores on my palm, "but if you could recommend something?"

"I've just the thing that might help." Tavey took my arm to lead me. We stopped along the berths while Tavey checked on a few of the other passengers before ending up at her cot.

She took out her bag and rummaged through it. "Whatever have you been doing, child?" she asked, glancing over at me.

"Chopping cabbages for the cook."

Tavey paused, her expression one of surprise. "Chopping cabbages gave you those?"

"There were an awful lot of cabbages," I defended, "over the last two days."

Inspired by the Celtic Knotwork of ancient times, the Eternal Knot has no beginning or end, thought to represent the uninterrupted cycle of life. Use this pattern to practice the Eternal Knot cable pattern before trying one of the larger projects in this book. Cadha's Capelet, and Thom's Cap & Mitts all use the same knotwork pattern.

Difficulty
Intermediate

Finished Size
6 ¼"(16cm) by 8"(20cm) body, 29"(74cm) strap

Yarn Used
Approx. 225yds(206m) Worsted Weight Yarn

Yarn used for sample: Alexandra's Crafts Depoe Bay, 100% Superwash Merino (220yds/201m, 2.5oz/71g)

Notions
- Size G/4mm crochet hook or hook to get gauge
- Stitch Marker(s)
- Tapestry Needle

Gauge
17 sts by 19 rows in sc = 4"(10cm)

PATTERN NOTES

- Hdc2tog is always made in next 2 stitches, unless other stitches are specified.
- When working behind stitches just made, pull them toward you to better see stitches being worked into.
- See Page 24 for additional Tips for Working Cables.
- If sl st round makes edging pucker or tighten up, try using one hook size larger than rest of project.

SPECIAL STITCHES

Front Post Double Crochet (fpdc): Yo, insert hook around post from front of indicated st, yo, pull up a loop, [yo, pull through 2 lps on hook] 2 times.

Front Post Treble Crochet (fptr): Yo 2 times, insert hook around post from front of indicated st, yo, pull up a loop, [yo, pull through 2 lps on hook] 3 times.

Front Post Double crochet 2 together (fpdc2tog): Yo, insert hook around post of first indicated st from front, yo, pull up a loop, yo, pull through 2 loops, skip indicated *sts*, yo, insert hook around post of next indicated st from front, yo, pull up a loop, yo, pull through 2 loops, yo, pull through all 3 loops on hook.

Back Post Double Crochet (bpdc): Yo, insert hook around post from back of indicated st *(see bottom photo)*, yo, pull up a loop, [yo, pull through 2 lps on hook] 2 times.

Back Post Treble Crochet (bptr): Yo 2 times, insert hook around post from back of indicated st, yo, pull up a loop, [yo, pull through 2 lps on hook] 3 times.

Back Post Double crochet 2 together (bpdc2tog): Yo, insert hook around post of first indicated st from back, yo, pull up a loop, yo, pull through 2 loops, *skip indicated sts*, yo, insert hook around post of next indicated st from back, yo, pull up a loop, yo, pull through 2 loops, yo, pull through all 3 loops on hook.

SATCHEL PATTERN

Front Panel
Ch 25.

Row 1 (WS): Hdc in second ch from hook and each ch across, turn. (24 hdc)

Rows 2: Ch 1 *(does not count as first hdc here and throughout)*, hdc in each hdc across, turn.

Row 3: Ch 1, hdc in first 9 hdc, hdc2tog, sk next hdc, fptr around next hdc; Working behind fptr just made, hdc in sk hdc, hdc in same hdc as prev fptr, fpdc around same hdc as prev fptr, hdc2tog, hdc in last 9 hdc, turn. *(See Tutorials on page 60 or 66 for Beginning an Eternal Knot Cable.)*

Row 4: Ch 1, hdc in first 8 hdc, hdc2tog, bpdc around next fpdc, bpdc around next hdc, hdc in same hdc as bpdc just made, hdc in next hdc, bptr around same hdc as prev bpdc, bpdc around next fptr, hdc2tog, hdc in last 8 hdc, turn.

Row 5: Ch 1, hdc in first 9 sts, fpdc around each of next 2 sts, hdc in next 2 hdc, fpdc around each of next 2 sts, hdc2tog in top of same st as fpdc just made and next hdc, hdc in last 8 hdc, turn.

Row 6: Ch 1, hdc in first 10 sts, bpdc around same fpdc as hdc just made, bpdc around next fpdc, sk 2 hdc, bpdc around each of next 2 fpdc, hdc in top of same st as bpdc just made, hdc in last 9 hdc, turn.

Row 7: Ch 1, hdc in first 3 hdc, *hdc2tog, sk next hdc, fptr around next hdc; Working behind fptr just made, hdc in sk hdc, hdc in same hdc as prev fptr, fpdc around same hdc as prev fptr, hdc2tog**, hdc2tog in next hdc and top of first bpdc, sk next bpdc, fptr around each of next 2 bpdc; Working in front of 2 sts just made, fptr around bpdc used in prev hdc2tog, fptr around sk bpdc *(first cross completed)*, hdc2tog in same st as second fptr of cross and next hdc; Rep * to **, hdc in last 3 hdc, turn. *(See Tutorials on page 61 or 67 for Crossed Cables.)*

Row 8: Ch 1, hdc in first 2 hdc, hdc2tog, *bpdc around next fpdc, bpdc around next hdc, hdc in same hdc as bpdc just made, hdc in next hdc, bptr around same hdc as prev bpdc, bpdc around next fptr**, sk 2 hdc2tog, bpdc around each of next 2 fptr, hdc in top of same fptr as prev st, hdc in next fptr, bpdc around same fptr as prev st, bpdc around next fptr, sk 2 hdc2tog; Rep * to **, hdc2tog, hdc in last 2 hdc, turn.

Row 9: Ch 1, hdc in first 3 sts, fpdc around each of next 2 sts, hdc in next hdc, *hdc2tog in next hdc and top of next bpdc, sk next bpdc, fptr around each of next 2 sts; Working behind 2 sts just made, fptr around bpdc used in hdc2tog, fptr around sk bpdc, hdc2tog in same st as second fptr of cross and next hdc;

Rep once from *, hdc in next hdc, fpdc around each of next 2 bpdc, hdc2tog in same st as fpdc just made and next hdc, hdc in last 2 hdc, turn.

Row 10: Ch 1, hdc in first 4 sts, *bpdc around same post st as hdc just made, bpdc around next post st, sk 2 sts, bpdc around each of next 2 post sts, hdc in top of same post st as bpdc just made**, hdc in next fptr; Rep once from *; Rep once from* to **, hdc in last 3 hdc, turn.

Row 11: Ch 1, hdc in first 3 hdc, *hdc2tog in next hdc and top of next bpdc, sk next bpdc, fptr around each of next 2 bpdc; Working in front of 2 bpdc just made, fptr around bpdc used in prev hdc2tog, fptr around sk bpdc, hdc2tog in same st as second fptr of cross and next hdc; Rep from * 2 more times, hdc in last 3 hdc, turn.

Row 12: Ch 1, hdc in first 2 hdc, hdc2tog in next hdc and next hdc2tog, *bpdc around

16

each of next 2 fptr, hdc in same fptr as st just made, hdc in next fptr, bpdc around same fptr as hdc just made, bpdc around next fptr**, sk 2 hdc2tog; Rep once from *; Rep * to **, hdc2tog in next hcd2tog and next hdc, hdc in last 2 hdc, turn.

Row 13: Ch 1, hdc in first 3 sts, fpdc around each of next 2 bpdc, hdc in next hdc, *hdc2tog in next hdc and top of next bpdc, sk next bpdc, fptr around each of next 2 bpdc, working behind 2 fptr just made, fptr around bpdc used in hdc2tog, fptr around sk bpdc, hdc2tog in same bpdc as second fptr of cross and next hdc; Rep once from *, hdc in next hdc, fpdc around each of next 2 bpdc, hdc2tog in same st as fpdc just made and next hdc2tog, hdc in last 2 hdc, turn.

Row 14: Ch 1, hdc in first 4 sts, bpdc around same st as hdc just made, bpdc2tog in next fpdc and next fptr *(skip 2 sts between, see Special Stitches)*, bpdc around next fptr, 2 hdc in top of same fptr as bpdc just made, hdc in next fptr, bpdc around same fptr as hdc just made, bpdc around next fptr, sk 2 sts, bpdc around each of next 2 fptr, hdc in same st as bpdc just made, 2 hdc in next fptr, bpdc around same fptr as 2 hdc just made, bpdc2tog in next fptr and next fpdc *(skip 2 sts between)*, bpdc around next fpdc, hdc in same st as bpdc just made, hdc in last 3 hdc, turn.

Row 15: Ch 1, hdc in first 5 sts, *fpdc2tog in same bpdc as hdc just made and next bpdc *(skip bpdc2tog between, see Special Stitches)*, hdc in second bpdc used for fpdc2tog**, hdc in next 2 hdc, hdc2tog in next hdc and next bpdc, sk 1 bpdc, fptr around each of next 2 bpdc, working in front of 2 fptr just made work fptr around bpdc used in hdc2tog, fptr around sk bpdc, hdc2tog in same st as second fptr of cross and next hdc,

hdc in next 3 sts; Rep * to **, hdc in last 4 hdc, turn.

Row 16: Ch 1, hdc in first 8 sts, hdc2tog, bpdc around each of next 2 fptr, hdc in same st as bpdc just made, hdc in next fptr, bpdc around same st as hdc just made, bpdc around next fptr, hdc2tog, hdc in last 8 sts, turn.

Row 17: Ch 1, hdc in first 9 sts, fpdc around each of next 2 bpdc, hdc in next 2 hdc, fpdc around each of next 2 bpdc, hdc2tog in same st as fpdc just made and next hdc2tog, hdc in last 8 hdc, turn.

Row 18: Ch 1, hdc in first 10 sts, bpdc around same fpdc as hdc just made, bpdc2tog in next 2 fpdc *(skip 2 sts between)*, bpdc around next fpdc, 2 hdc in top of same st as bpdc just made, hdc in last 9 hdc, turn.

Row 19: Ch 1, hdc in first 12 sts, fpdc2tog in same bpdc as hdc just made and next bpdc *(skip bpdc2tog between)*, hdc in second bpdc used for fpdc2tog, hdc in last 10 hdc, turn.

Rows 20-21: Ch 1, hdc in each st across, turn. Place stitch marker in top of last stitch of last row.

Row 22: Ch 1, hdc in each st across, turn.

Body of Bag
Rows 23-57: Ch 1, sc in each st across, turn. Place stitch marker in top of last stitch of last row.

Rows 58-92: Ch 1, sc in each st across, turn. Do not finish off.

Tips for Working Evenly Around Edges
• Work 1 st in side of every row of sc. • Work 3 sts in sides of every 2 rows of hdc. • Insert hook into 2 loops of sides of sts.

Edging

Rnd 1: Work into last row of body with RS facing, ch 1, *2 sc in first st, sc in next 22 sts, 2 sc in corner st; Turn to work across sides of rows, 2 sc in side of first row; Work approx. 103 sc evenly across to next corner, 2 sc in side of last row**; Turn to work into unused loops of chs along beginning end, Rep * to **, 2 sc in same st as first sc, join with sl st in first sc – 262 sc. *(Note: Your stitch count on sides may vary, be sure to count them so you have the same number of stitches on both sides.)*

Rnd 2: Sl st in each sc across bottom edge. Finish off – 26 sl st.

FINISHING

Seaming

With WS facing, fold front of bag up so last row of sc meets last row of hdc on back, where stitch marker was placed. Hold in place with the stitch marker placed at the end of Row 22. Turn RS facing, join with sl st in sc at fold of bottom corner.

Row 1: Seam front and back of body together with sl sts through both sides in each sc up to stitch marker, continue to sl st *loosely (see*

Pattern Notes) in each sc and ch around Front Panel; Careful to join front to back at the same point, continue to sl st in each sc down side, working through both front and back of bag. Finish off.

Strap

Join with sl st near side seam at base of Front Panel, ch 110, careful not to twist, join with sl st near side seam on other side of panel, sl st in corner edge of front, turn.

Row 1: Hdc in back bump of each ch, sl st in corner edge of front, turn.

Row 2: With top of strap facing, sl st in top of each st across, sl st in top of side seam, turn.

Row 3: Sl st in unused loops of beg ch across strap, sl st in other side. Finish off and weave in all ends, using ends of yarn to anchor strap more securely.

Blocking

Use steam iron to block Strap and Front Flap. Pin fabric to while damp to smooth edges and allow it to dry.

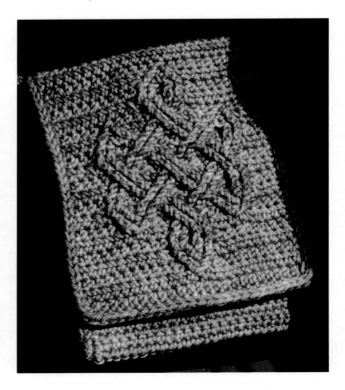

Alternative Design Ideas
- Add a Closure by adding a Chain Button Loop to the bottom of the front flap.
- Or attach a Large Snap or Magnet Closure to the inside of the flap.
- Make a Longer Strap by adding more chains to the length, if you have additional yarn.
- Work up in a non-superwash wool on a larger hook and Felt it in your washer. Dry flat and trim around edges of cables with sharp scissors to make them pop.

ᴇTERNAL ᴋNOT ᴓTITCH ᴅIAGRAM

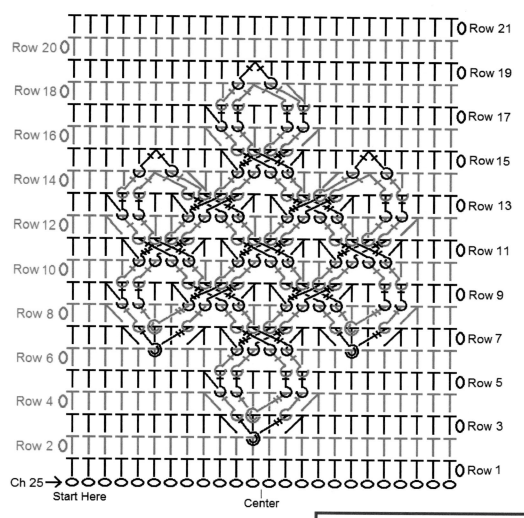

Row 21
Row 20
Row 19
Row 18
Row 17
Row 16
Row 15
Row 14
Row 13
Row 12
Row 11
Row 10
Row 9
Row 8
Row 7
Row 6
Row 5
Row 4
Row 3
Row 2
Row 1
Ch 25 →
Start Here
Center

Reading the Stitch Diagram

- Black rows are worked on RS of work (right to left for Right-handed crocheters/left to right for Left-handers).
- Blue rows are worked on WS, back in the other direction with WS facing you.
- The number of bars on the taller (dc & tr) stitches indicate how many times you will yarn over before inserting your hook.

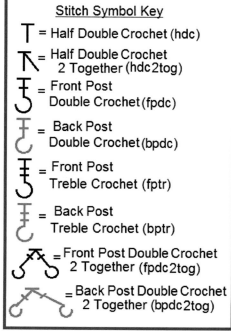

Stitch Symbol Key

T = Half Double Crochet (hdc)

⋏ = Half Double Crochet 2 Together (hdc2tog)

= Front Post Double Crochet (fpdc)

= Back Post Double Crochet (bpdc)

= Front Post Treble Crochet (fptr)

= Back Post Treble Crochet (bptr)

= Front Post Double Crochet 2 Together (fpdc2tog)

= Back Post Double Crochet 2 Together (bpdc2tog)

19

CADHA'S CELTIC CAPELET

Cadha joined us, and I was startled to see her dressed finely as well. After seeing her only in her working dresses, I hadn't realized how handsome she was. She must have been lovely in her youth. Her dress was primrose purple with a deep green trim close in color to my own skirts. She had no bonnet or mobcap, but instead had drawn a knitted capelet around her shoulders over her own cape and drawn the hood over her upswept graying hair. It buttoned under her chin with a simple hand-carved wooden button. The capelet was as rich of green as my skirts, too, and I noticed with some envy the fanciful Celtic knotwork stitched on the back. It looked warm, and I wished I had the skill to make one for myself. Perhaps she could teach me.

A modern interpretation of Cadha's Capelet worked in one continuous piece from the point of the hood down to the bottom edge. The pattern comes with three variations: a hood, an easy version without the cable, or a collar rather than a hood.

Difficulty
Experienced (with Knot); or Advanced Beginner (without knot)

Finished Size
With hood – 21"(53 ½cm) high by 22"(56cm) wide
Without – 12 ½"(32cm) high by 25"(63 ½cm) wide
Neck between 10 ½"(26 ½cm) to 12"(30 ½cm)

Yarn Used
Approx. 580yds(530m) Worsted Weight Yarn.

Yarn used in samples: DragynKnyts Wyrm, 100% Targhee Wool (580yds/530m, 8 oz/227g)

Notions
- Size K/6.5mm crochet hook or hook to get gauge
- Stitch Marker(s)
- One 1"(2 ½cm) to 1 ½"(4cm) wooden buttons from Craftwich Creations
- Coordinating Thread
- Tapestry and Sewing Needles

Gauge (before blocking)
12 sts by 10 rows in hdc = 4" (10cm); Rnds 1-7 of Hood folded flat = 4"(10cm) across and 3"(7 ¾cm) from point to center

PATTERN NOTES

- Use a stitch marker to mark the first hdc in the Hood rounds. Move it up with each round to keep track when working in continuous rounds.
- Hdc2tog is always made over next 2 stitches, unless other stitches are specified.
- When working behind stitches just made, pull them toward you to better see stitches being worked into.
- If you have not tried the crocheted cables before, practice by beginning with the Knotwork Panel in Tavey's Satchel Pattern (on page 14).
- If sl st round makes edging pucker or tighten up, try using one hook size larger than rest of project.

SPECIAL STITCHES *(Additional post stitches for cables on page 15)*

Reverse Slip Knot: Form beginning slip knot with adjustable side of knot attached to short end rather than attached to the ball of yarn *(see Tutorials on page 58 or 64)*. This is an alternative to starting with a "magic circle" or "adjustable ring".

CAPELET PATTERNS:

CAPELET WITH HOOD

Hood

Form a reverse slip knot *(see Special Stitches and Tutorials on page 58 or 64)* or magic ring.

Rnd 1: Ch 2, 4 hdc in first ch (or ring), pull ring tight, do not join. Use a stitch marker to mark the first hdc in rnd. Work Hood in continuous rounds. (4 hdc)

Rnd 2: 2 hdc each hdc around. (8 hdc)

Rnd 3: [2 hdc in next hdc, hdc in next hdc] around. (12 hdc)

Rnd 4: [2 hdc in next hdc, hdc in next 2 hdc] around. (16 hdc)

Rnd 5: [2 hdc in next hdc, hdc in next 3 hdc] around. (20 hdc)

Rnd 6: [2 hdc in next hdc, hdc in next 4 hdc] around. (24 hdc)

Rnd 7: [2 hdc in next hdc, hdc in next 5 hdc] around. (28 hdc)

Rnd 8: [2 hdc in next hdc, hdc in next 6 hdc] around. (32 hdc)

Rnd 9: [2 hdc in next hdc, hdc in next 7 hdc] around. (36 hdc)

Rnd 10: [2 hdc in next hdc, hdc in next 8 hdc] around. (40 hdc)

Rnd 11: [2 hdc in next hdc, hdc in next 9 hdc] around. (44 hdc)

Rnd 12: [2 hdc in next hdc, hdc in next 10 hdc] around. (48 hdc)

Rnd 13: [2 hdc in next hdc, hdc in next 11 hdc] around. (52 hdc)

Rnd 14: [2 hdc in next hdc, hdc in next 12 hdc] around. (56 hdc)

Rnd 15: [2 hdc in next hdc, hdc in next 13 hdc] around. (60 hdc)

Rnd 16: [2 hdc in next hdc, hdc in next 14 hdc] around. (64 hdc)

Rnd 17: [2 hdc in next hdc, hdc in next 15 hdc] around. (68 hdc)

Rnd 18: [2 hdc in next hdc, hdc in next 16 hdc] around. (72 hdc)

Rnd 19: [2 hdc in next hdc, hdc in next 17 hdc] around. (76 hdc)

Rnd 20: [2 hdc in next hdc, hdc in next 18 hdc] around. (80 hdc)

Rnd 21: Hdc in first 30 hdc, 3 hdc in next hdc, hdc in next 48 hdc, 3 hdc in next hdc. (84 hdc)

Rnd 22: Hdc in first 31 hdc, 3 hdc in next hdc, hdc in next 51 hdc, 3 hdc in next hdc. (88 hdc)

Rnd 23: Hdc in first 32 hdc, 3 hdc in next hdc, hdc in next 54 hdc, 3 hdc in next hdc. (92 hdc)

Rnd 24: Hdc in first 33 hdc, 3 hdc in next hdc, hdc in next 57 hdc, 3 hdc in next hdc. (96 hdc)

Rnd 25: Hdc in first 34 hdc, 3 hdc in next hdc, hdc in next 60 hdc, 3 hdc in next hdc. (100 hdc)

Rnd 26: Hdc in first 35 hdc, 3 hdc in next hdc, hdc in next 63 hdc, 3 hdc in next hdc. (104 hdc)

Tips for Working Cable Rows
- Refer to Stitch Diagram to be sure you are inserting into or around the correct stitches.
- Remember the post stitches in each row will be either all front post (when RS facing) or all back post (when WS facing).
- On WS rows, be careful not to skip the first part of the crossed cables as they can become hidden between the other stitches.

Rnd 27: Hdc in first 36 hdc, 3 hdc in next hdc, hdc in next 66 hdc, 3 hdc in next hdc. (108 hdc) Do not finish, continue with Cape.

Cape

Row 1: Sc in first 40 hdc, leave remaining hdc unworked, turn. (40 sc)

Row 2: Ch 2 (does not count as first hdc here and throughout), hdc in first hdc, [2 hdc in next hdc, hdc in next 2 sc] 13 times; Working into unused hdc of last rnd of Hood, hdc in next hdc, 2 hdc in next hdc, leave remaining sts unworked, turn. (56 hdc)

Row 3: Ch 2, hdc in first hdc, [2 hdc in next hdc, hdc in next 5 hdc] 9 times, 2 hdc in last hdc, turn. (66 hdc)]

Row 4: Ch 2, [hdc in first 10 hdc, 2 hdc in next hdc] 6 times, turn. (72 hdc)

Row 5: Ch 2, [hdc in first 8 hdc, 2 hdc in next hdc] 8 times, turn. (80 hdc)

Row 6: Ch 2, [hdc in first 7 hdc, 2 hdc in next hdc] 10 times. Do not turn. Place stitch markers in stitches 13, 30, 46, 61, and 78, to indicate where to increase and start cables. Turn now. (90 hdc)

For Easy version, follow Plain Capelet instructions on page 27 for Rows 7-24.

(Follow Knotwork Panel diagram on page 19, beginning at Row 3 of diagram.)

Row 7: Ch 1, hdc in first 12, 2 hdc in next hdc, hdc in next 16 hdc, 2 hdc in next hdc, hdc in next 12 hdc, hdc2tog, sk next hdc, fptr around next hdc; Working behind fptr just made, hdc in sk hdc, hdc in same hdc as prev fptr, fpdc around same hdc as prev fptr, hdc2tog, hdc in next 12 hdc, 2 hdc in next hdc, hdc in next 16 hdc, 2 hdc in next hdc, hdc in next 11 hdc, 2 hdc in last hdc, turn. (95 sts) *(See Tutorials on page 60 or 66 for Beginning an Eternal Knot Cable.)*

Row 8: Ch 1, hdc in first 13 hdc, 2 hdc in next hdc, hdc in next 17 hdc, 2 hdc in next hdc, hdc in next 12 hdc, hdc2tog, bpdc around next fpdc, bpdc around next hdc, hdc in same hdc as bpdc, hdc in next hdc, bptr around same hdc as prev bpdc, bpdc around next fptr, hdc2tog, hdc in next 11 hdc, 2 hdc in next hdc, hdc in next 17 hdc, 2 hdc in next hdc, hdc in next 12 hdc, 2 hdc in last hdc, turn. (100 hdc)

Row 9: Ch 1, hdc in first 14 hdc, 2 hdc in next hdc, hdc in next 18 hdc, 2 hdc in next hdc, hdc in next 13 hdc, fpdc around each of next 2 sts, hdc in next 2 hdc, fpdc around each of next 2 sts, hdc2tog in top of same st as fpdc just made and next hdc, hdc in next 12 hdc, 2 hdc in next hdc, hdc in next 18 hdc, 2 hdc in next hdc, hdc in next 13 hdc, 2 hdc in last hdc, turn. (105 hdc)

25

Row 10: Ch 1, hdc in first 15 hdc, 2 hdc in next hdc, hdc in next 19 hdc, 2 hdc in next hdc, hdc in next 15 sts, bpdc around same fpdc as hdc just made, bpdc around next fpdc, sk 2 hdc, bpdc around each of next 2 fpdc, hdc in top of same st as st just made, hdc in next 13 hdc, 2 hdc in next hdc, hdc in next 19 hdc, 2 hdc in next hdc, hdc in next 14 hdc, 2 hdc in last hdc, turn. (110 hdc)

Row 11: Ch 1, hdc in first 16 hdc, 2 hdc in next hdc, hdc in next 20 hdc, 2 hdc in next hdc, hdc in next 8 hdc, *hdc2tog, sk next hdc, fptr around next hdc; Working behind fptr just made, hdc in sk hdc, hdc in same hdc as prev fptr, fpdc around same hdc as fptr, hdc2tog**, hdc2tog in next hdc and top of first bpdc, sk next bpdc, fptr around each of next 2 bpdc; Working in front of 2 sts just made, fptr around bpdc used in hdc2tog, fptr around sk bpdc *(first cross completed)*, hdc2tog in same st as second fptr of cross and next hdc; Rep * to **, hdc in next 8 hdc, 2 hdc in next hdc, hdc in next 20 hdc, 2 hdc in next hdc, hdc in next 15 hdc, 2 hdc in last hdc, turn. (115 hdc) *(See Tutorials on page 61 or 67 for Crossed Cables.)*

Row 12: Ch 1, hdc in first 17 hdc, 2 hdc in next hdc, hdc in next 21 hdc, 2 hdc in next hdc, hdc in next 8 hdc, hdc2tog, *bpdc around next fpdc, bpdc around next hdc, hdc in same hdc as st just made, hdc in next hdc, bptr around same hdc as prev bpdc, bpdc around next fptr**, sk 2 hdc2tog, bpdc around each of next 2 fptr, hdc in top of same fptr as st just made, hdc in next fptr, bpdc around same fptr as st just made, bpdc around next fptr, sk 2 hdc2tog; Rep * to **, hdc2tog, hdc in next 8 hdc, 2 hdc in next hdc, hdc in next 21 hdc, 2 hdc in next hdc, hdc in next 16 hdc, 2 hdc in last hdc, turn. (120 hdc)

Row 13: Ch 1, hdc in first 18 hdc, 2 hdc in next hdc, hdc in next 22 hdc, 2 hdc in next hdc, hdc in next 9 sts, fpdc around each of next 2 sts, hdc in next hdc, *hdc2tog in next hdc and top of next bpdc, sk next bpdc, fptr around each of next 2 sts; Working behind 2 sts just made, fptr around second bpdc used in hdc2tog, fptr around sk bpdc, hdc2tog in same st as second fptr of cross and next hdc; Rep once from *, hdc in next hdc, fpdc around each of next 2 bpdc, hdc2tog in same st as fpdc just made and next hdc, hdc in next 8 hdc, 2 hdc in next hdc, hdc in next 22 hdc, 2 hdc in next hdc, hdc in next 17 hdc, 2 hdc in last hdc, turn. (125 hdc)

Row 14: Ch 1, hdc in first 54 sts, hdc first fpdc, *bpdc around same post st as hdc just made, bpdc around next post st, sk 2 sts, bpdc around each of next 2 post sts, hdc in top of same post st as bpdc just made**, hdc in next fptr; Rep once from *; Rep once from * to **, hdc in next 52 hdc, 2 hdc in last hdc, turn. (126 hdc)

Row 15: Ch 1, hdc in first 20 hdc, 2 hdc in next hdc, hdc in next 23 hdc, 2 hdc in next hdc, hdc in next 9 hdc, *hdc2tog in next hdc and top of next bpdc, sk next bpdc, fptr around each of next 2 bpdc; Working in front of 2 sts just made, fptr around bpdc used in hdc2tog, fptr around sk bpdc, hdc2tog in same st as second fptr of cross and next hdc; Rep from * 2 more times, hdc in next 9 hdc, 2 hdc in next hdc, hdc in next 23 hdc, 2 hdc in next hdc, hdc in next 19 hdc, 2 hdc in last hdc, turn. (131 hdc)

Row 16: Ch 1, hdc in first 56 hdc, hdc2tog in next hdc and next hdc2tog, *bpdc around each of next 2 fptr, hdc in same fptr as st just made, hdc in next fptr, bpdc around same fptr as hdc just made, bpdc around next fptr**, sk 2 hdc2tog; Rep once from *; Rep * to **, hdc2tog in next hcd2tog and next hdc, hdc in

26

next 54 hdc, 2 hdc in last hdc, turn. (132 hdc)

Row 17: Ch 1, hdc in first 57 sts, fpdc around each of next 2 bpdc, hdc in next hdc, *hdc2tog in next hdc and top of next bpdc, sk next bpdc, fptr around each of next 2 bpdc, working behind 2 sts just made' work fptr around bpdc used in hdc2tog, fptr around sk bpdc, hdc2tog in same st as fptr of cross and next hdc; Rep once from *, hdc in next hdc, fpdc around each of next 2 bpdc, hdc2tog in same st as fpdc just made and next hdc2tog, hdc in next 55 hdc, 2 hdc in last hdc, turn. (133 hdc)

Row 18: Ch 1, hdc in first 59 sts, bpdc around same st as hdc just made, bpdc2tog over next fpdc and next fptr *(skip 2 sts between, see Special Stitches on page 15)*, bpdc around next fptr, 2 hdc in top of same fptr as bpdc just made, hdc in next fptr, bpdc around same fptr as hdc just made, bpdc around next fptr, sk 2 hdc2tog, bpdc around each of next 2 fptr, hdc in same st as bpdc just made, 2 hdc in next fptr, bpdc around same fptr as 2 hdc just made, bpdc2tog over next fptr and next fpdc *(skip 2 sts between)*, bpdc around next fpdc, hdc in same st as bpdc just made, hdc in next 56 hdc, 2 hdc in last hdc, turn. (134 sts)

Row 19: Ch 1, hdc in first 60 sts, *fpdc2tog over same bpdc as hdc just made and next bpdc *(skip bpdc2tog between, see Special Stitches on page 15)*, hdc in second bpdc used for fpdc2tog**, hdc in next 2 hdc, hdc2tog in next hdc and next bpdc, sk 1 bpdc, fptr around each of next 2 bpdc, working in front of 2 sts just made work fptr around bpdc used in hdc2tog, fptr around sk bpdc, hdc2tog in same st as second fptr of cross and next hdc, hdc in next 3 sts; Rep * to **, hdc in next 58 hdc, 2 hdc in last hdc, turn. (135 sts)

Row 20: Ch 1, hdc in first 64 hdc, hdc2tog, bpdc around each of next 2 fptr, hdc in same st as bpdc just made, hdc in next fptr, bpdc around same st as hdc just made, bpdc around next fptr, hdc2tog, hdc in next 62 hdc, 2 hdc in last hdc, turn. (136 sts)

Row 21: Ch 1, hdc in first 65 sts, fpdc around each of next 2 bpdc, hdc in next 2 hdc, fpdc around each of next 2 bpdc, hdc2tog in same st as st just made and next hdc2tog, hdc in next 63 hdc, 2 hdc in last hdc, turn. (137 sts)

Row 22: Ch 1, hdc in first 67 sts, bpdc around same fpdc as hdc just made, bpdc2tog over next 2 fpdc *(skip 2 sts between)*, bpdc around next fpdc, 2 hdc in top of same st as bpdc just made, hdc in next 64 hdc, 2 hdc in last hdc, turn. (138 sts)

Row 23: Ch 1, hdc in first 69 sts, fpdc2tog over same bpdc as hdc just made and next bpdc *(skip bpdc2tog between)*, hdc in second bpdc used for fpdc2tog, hdc in next 66 hdc, 2 hdc in last hdc, turn. (139 sts)

Row 24: Ch 1, hdc in first 138 hdc, 2 hdc in last hdc, turn. (140 sts)

Edging

Rnd 1: Continuing from Row 24, ch 1, sc in each hdc across to last hdc of bottom edge, 3 sc in corner st, sc evenly around edges of sides and hood, 2 sc in second corner, join with sl st in first sc. *(See Tips for Working Evenly Around Edges on page 17.)*

Rnd 2: Sl st in each sc around. Finish off.

PLAIN CAPELET

WITHOUT KNOT − *Option 2*
(Easy - Sample not shown)

Follow instructions for Hooded Capelet up to Row 6 of Cape. Then follow instructions on next page for rows 7 on.

Row 7: Ch 1, hdc in first 12 hdc, *2 hdc in next hdc, hdc in next 16 hdc, 2 hdc in next hdc**, hdc in next 30 sc; Rep * to **, hdc in next 11, 2 hdc in last hdc, turn. (95 hdc)

Row 8: Ch 1, hdc in first 13 hdc, *2 hdc in next hdc, hdc in next 17 hdc, 2 hdc in next hdc**, hdc in next 31 hdc; Rep * to **, hdc in next 12 hdc, 2 hdc in last hdc, turn. (100 hdc)

Row 9: Ch 1, hdc in first 14 hdc, *2 hdc in next hdc, hdc in next 18 hdc, 2 hdc in next hdc**, hdc in next 32 hdc; Rep * to **, hdc in next 13 hdc, 2 hdc in last hdc, turn. (105 hdc)

Row 10: Ch 1, hdc in first 15 hdc, *2 hdc in next hdc, hdc in next 19, 2 hdc in next hdc**, hdc in next 33 hdc; Rep * to **, hdc in next 14 hdc, 2 hdc in last hdc, turn. (110 hdc)

Row 11: Ch 1, hdc in first 16 hdc, *2 hdc in

next hdc, hdc in next 20 hdc, 2 hdc in next hdc**, hdc in next 34 hdc; Rep * to **, hdc in next 15 hdc, 2 hdc in last hdc, turn. (115 hdc)

Row 12: Ch 1, hdc in first 17 hdc, *2 hdc in next hdc, hdc in next 21 hdc, 2 hdc in next hdc**, hdc in next 35 hdc; Rep * to **, hdc in next 16 hdc, 2 hdc in last hdc, turn. (120 hdc)

Row 13: Ch 1, hdc in first 18 hdc, *2 hdc in next hdc, hdc in next 22 hdc, 2 hdc in next hdc**, hdc in next 36 hdc; Rep * to **, hdc in next 17 hdc, 2 hdc in last hdc, turn. (125 hdc)

Row 14: Ch 1, hdc in each st around, 2 hdc in last hdc, turn. (126 hdc)

Row 15: Ch 1, hdc in first 20 hdc, *2 hdc in next hdc, hdc in next 24 hdc, 2 hdc in next hdc**, hdc in next 36 hdc; Rep * to **, hdc in next 19 hdc, 2 hdc in last hdc, turn. (131 hdc)

Rows 16-24: Repeat Row 14. Increasing 1 hdc per row, ending with 140 hdc. Do not finish off.

Edging Rnd: Ch 1, sc in each hdc across to last hdc of bottom edge, 3 sc in corner st, sc evenly around edges of sides and hood, 2 sc in second corner, join with sl st in first sc. Finish off. *(See Tips for Working Evenly Around Edges on page 17.)*

CAPELET WITH COLLAR
WITHOUT HOOD - *Option 3*

Chain 41.

Row 1: Sc in second ch from hook and each ch across, turn. (40 sc)

Row 2: Ch 2 (does not count as first hdc here and throughout), 2 hdc in first hdc, [2 hdc in next hdc, hdc in next 2 sc] 12 times, 2 hdc in each of next 3 sc, turn. (56 hdc)

Rows 3-24: Rows 3-24 of Capelet With Hood.

Rows 25-28: Repeat Row 24 of Capelet With Hood.

First-Side Collar
Work along neckline in unused loops of beg chain of Cape. With WS (back of cables) facing, join with standing hdc in unused loops of first chain *(on right-side for right-handed crochers or left-side for left-handed)*.

Row 1: Hdc in same ch as join, hdc in next ch, [hdc in next 5 ch, 2 hdc in next ch] 3 times, leave remaining sts unworked, turn. (24 hdc)

Row 2: Ch 1, 2 hdc in first hdc, hdc in next hdc, [2 hdc in next hdc, hdc in next 2 hdc] 6 times, turn. (32 hdc)

Row 3: Ch 1, hdc in first hdc, [hdc in next 4 hdc, 2 hdc in next hdc] 5 times, hdc in next 3 hdc, 2 hdc in last hdc, turn. (38 hdc)

Row 4: Ch 1, hdc in each hdc across to last hdc, 2 hdc in last hdc, turn. (39 hdc)

Row 5: Ch 1, hdc2tog in first 2 hdc, hdc in each hdc across to last 2 hdc, hdc2tog, turn. (37 hdc)

Row 6: Ch 1, hdc2tog in first 2 hdc, hdc in each hdc across to last 3 hdc, hdc2tog, leave last hdc2tog unworked. Finish off. (34 hdc)

Second-Side Collar
With WS facing, join with standing hdc in unused loops of next chain left unworked from First-Side. Repeat Rows 1-6 of First Side.

Edging
Rnd 1: With RS facing, join in first hdc of last row of Cape. Ch 1, sc in each hdc across to last hdc, 3 hdc in last hdc, turn to work up first side, work 44 sc evenly into sides of sts on first side to base of neck *(see Tips on page 17)*, 53 sc around second side of Collar, sl st in 2 center sts at back of neck between two sides of Collar, 53 sc around next side of Collar, 44 sc down second side of Cape, 2 sc in same hdc as first sc at corner, join with sl st in first sc.

Rnd 2: Sl st in each sc around. Finish off and weave in ends.

FINISHING

Blocking
Use iron or fabric steamer to steam block capelet to smooth fabric and add drape. Sew on button loop with yarn and tapestry needle.

Trinity Knot Button Loop
Chain 33, inserting hook under 2 loops of chs, sl st in second ch from hook and each ch across. Fasten off leaving 1 yard long end for sewing. Weave strand into Trinity Knot as shown in photo. With yarn needle, sew center and two loops of knot onto one side of front, leaving one loop for the buttonhole.

Button
With sewing needle and thread, sew button onto other side of front. Insert needle through several strands of yarn from different directions to avoid pulling on yarn.

T
H
O
M
'
S

C
A
P

&

M
I
T
T
S

"You go with Thom," Cadha told me.

I looked where she gestured to see Thom standing at the other end of the barn by a second set of doors. He had pulled on a woolen knit hat and looked to be wearing a pair of matching mittens, along with his warmest coat.

Create smaller Eternal Knot cables to adorn this simple half double crochet hat and fingerless mitts. Worked with DK weight yarn on a smaller size hook, you can use the same knotwork pattern as the Satchel and Capelet to create these detailed knots.

Difficulty: Experienced

Finished Size
Cap: 7"(18cm) tall, 19"(48cm) circ.
Mitts: 7 ½"(19cm) tall, 6 ½"(15 ½cm) circ.
(See Adjusting Patterns for Size and Fit box on page 39 for ways to change size.)

Yarn
400yds(366m) DK weight yarn (approx. 200yds/183m each for Cap or Mitts)

Yarn used for sample: Stitchjones Buenos Aires, 85% Polwarth wool, 15% silk (290yds/265m, 100g/3.53oz), 2 skeins in Simpson Desert

Notions
• E/3.5mm hook or size needed to obtain gauge
• Tapestry needle

Gauge
18 sts by 16 rows in hdc = 4"(10cm); Rnds 1- 7 of Hat Pattern = 3 ¾"(9 ½cm) diameter

PATTERN NOTES

- Join and turn at end of each round in order to complete cable pattern worked back and forth rather than in continuous rounds.
- After turning, DO NOT work into the slip stitch. Work first stitch of each round into the first half double crochet, unless slip stitch is specified on increase rounds.
- Hdc2tog is always made over next 2 stitches, unless other stitches are specified.
- When working behind stitches just made, pull them toward you to better see stitches being worked into.
- See Page 24 for additional Tips for Working Cables.
- If you have not tried the crocheted cables before, practice by beginning with the Knotwork Panel in Tavey's Satchel Pattern (on page 14).
- In the mitt pattern, instructions in parenthesis indicate number of stitches to work for second mitt (left mitt for right-handed crocheters and right mitt for left-handed crocheters).

SPECIAL STITCHES (additional post stitches for Cables on page 15)

Working in the Back Bump – Insert hook in the hump on the back of each chain stitch rather than the loops of the "v" on the front. *(See Tutorials on page 58 or 64 for Back Bump.)*

Single Crochet 2 Together (sc2tog) – *Insert hook into next st, yo, pull up a loop (2 loops on hook); Repeat from *, yo, pull through all 3 loops on hook.

Half Double Crochet 2 Together (hdc2tog) – *Yo, insert hook into next st, yo, pull up a loop (3 loops on hook); Repeat from *, yo, pull through all 5 loops on hook.

HAT PATTERN

Form a reverse slip knot *(see Tutorials on page 58 or 64)*, ch 2.

Rnd 1: 8 hdc in second ch from hook *(or adjustable ring)*, pull ring tight, join with sl st in first hdc, turn. (8 hdc)

Rnd 2: Ch 1, hdc in first sl st, 2 hdc in next 7 hdc, hdc in last hdc (same st as join from prev rnd), join with sl st in first hdc, turn. (16 hdc)

Rnd 3: Ch 1, hdc in first sl st, hdc in next hdc, [2 hdc in next hdc, hdc in next hdc] 7 times, hdc in last hdc, join with sl st in first hdc, turn. (24 hdc)

Rnd 4: Ch 1, hdc in first sl st, hdc in next 2 hdc, [2 hdc in next hdc, hdc in next 2 hdc] 7 times, hdc in last hdc, join with sl st in first hdc, turn. (32 hdc)

Rnd 5: Ch 1, hdc in first sl st, hdc in next 3 hdc, [2 hdc in next hdc, hdc in next 3 hdc] 7 times, hdc in last hdc, join with sl st in first hdc, turn. (40 hdc)

Rnd 6: Ch 1, hdc in first sl st, hdc in next 4 hdc, [2 hdc in next hdc, hdc in next 4 hdc] 7 times, hdc in last hdc, join with sl st in first hdc, turn. (48 hdc)

Rnd 7: Ch 1, hdc in first sl st, hdc in next 5 hdc, [2 hdc in next hdc, hdc in next 5 hdc] 7 times, hdc in last hdc, join with sl st in first hdc, turn. (56 hdc)

Rnd 8: Ch 1, hdc in first sl st, hdc in next 6 hdc, [2 hdc in next hdc, hdc in next 6 hdc] 7 times, hdc in last hdc, join with sl st in first hdc, turn. (64 hdc)

Rnd 9: Ch 1, hdc in first sl st, hdc in next 7 hdc, [2 hdc in next hdc, hdc in next 7 hdc] 7 times, hdc in last hdc, join with sl st in first hdc, turn. (72 hdc)

Rnd 10: Ch 1, hdc in first sl st, hdc in next 8 hdc, [2 hdc in next hdc, hdc in next 8 hdc] 7 times, hdc in last hdc, join with sl st in first hdc, turn. (80 hdc)

(Follow Knotwork Panel diagram on page 19, beginning at Row 3 of diagram.)

Rnd 11: Ch 1, hdc in first sl st, [hdc in next 9 hdc, 2 hdc in next hdc] 2 times, hdc in next hdc, hdc2tog, sk next hdc, fptr around next hdc; Working behind fptr just made, hdc in sk hdc, hdc in same hdc as prev fptr, fpdc around same hdc as prev fptr, hdc2tog, hdc in next 2 hdc, [2 hdc in next hdc, hdc in next 9 hdc] 5 times, hdc in last hdc, join with sl st in first hdc, turn. (88 hdc) *(See Tutorials on page 60 or 66 for Beginning an Eternal Knot Cable.)*

Rnd 12: Ch 1, hdc in first 57 hdc, hdc2tog, bpdc around next fpdc, bpdc around next hdc, hdc in same hdc as bpdc, hdc in next hdc, bptr around same hdc as prev bpdc, bpdc around next fptr, hdc2tog, hdc in last 23 hdc, join with sl st in first hdc, turn.

Rnd13: Ch 1, hdc in first 24 sts, fpdc around each of next 2 sts, hdc in next 2 hdc, fpdc around each of next 2 sts, hdc2tog in top of same st as fpdc just made and next hdc, hdc in last 57 hdc, join with sl st in first hdc, turn.

Rnd 14: Ch 1, hdc in first 59 sts, bpdc around same fpdc as hdc just made, bpdc around next fpdc, sk 2 hdc, bpdc around each of next 2 fpdc, hdc in top of same st as st just made, hdc in last 24 hdc, join with sl st in first hdc, turn.

Rnd 15: Ch 1, hdc in first 18 hdc, *hdc2tog, sk next hdc, fptr around next hdc; Working **behind** fptr just made, hdc in sk hdc, hdc in same hdc as prev fptr, fpdc around same hdc as fptr, hdc2tog**, hdc2tog in next hdc and top of first bpdc, sk next bpdc, fptr around each of next 2 bpdc; Working in **front** of 2 sts just made, fptr around bpdc used in hdc2tog, fptr around sk bpdc *(first cross completed)*, hdc2tog in same st as second fptr of cross and next hdc; Rep * to **, hdc in last 52 hdc, join with sl st in first hdc, turn. *(See Tutorials on page 61 or 67 for Crossed Cables.)*

Rnd 16: Ch 1, hdc in first 51 hdc, hdc2tog, *bpdc around next fpdc, bpdc around next hdc, hdc in same hdc as st just made, hdc in next hdc, bptr around same hdc as prev bpdc, bpdc around next fptr**, sk 2 hdc2tog, bpdc around each of next 2 fptr, hdc in top of same fptr as st just made, hdc in next fptr, bpdc around same fptr as st just made, bpdc around next fptr, sk 2 hdc2tog; Rep * to **, hdc2tog, hdc in last 17 hdc, join with sl st in first hdc, turn.

Rnd 17: Ch 1, hdc in first 18 sts, fpdc around each of next 2 sts, hdc in next hdc, *hdc2tog in next hdc and top of next bpdc, sk next bpdc, fptr around each of next 2 sts; Working behind 2 sts just made, fptr around bpdc used in hdc2tog, fptr around sk bpdc, hdc2tog in same st as second fptr of cross and next hdc; Rep once from *, hdc in next hdc, fpdc around each of next 2 bpdc, hdc2tog in same st as fpdc just made and next hdc, hdc in last 51 hdc, join with sl st in first hdc, turn.

Rnd 18: Ch 1, hdc in first 53 sts, hdc first fpdc, *bpdc around same post st as hdc just made, bpdc around next post st, sk 2 hdc, bpdc around each of next 2 post sts, hdc in top of same post st as bpdc just made**, hdc in next fptr; Rep once from *; Rep once from* to **, hdc in last 18 hdc, join with sl st

in first hdc, turn.

Rnd 19: Ch 1, hdc in first 18 hdc, *hdc2tog in next hdc and top of next bpdc, sk next bpdc, fptr around each of next 2 bpdc; Working in front of 2 sts just made, fptr around bpdc used in hdc2tog, fptr around sk bpdc, hdc2tog in same st as second fptr of cross and next hdc; Rep from * 2 more times, hdc in last 52 hdc, join with sl st in first hdc, turn.

Rnd 20: Ch 1, hdc in first 51 hdc, hdc2tog in next hdc and next hdc2tog, *bpdc around each of next 2 fptr, hdc in same fptr as st just made, hdc in next fptr, bpdc around same fptr as hdc just made, bpdc around next fptr**, sk 2 hdc2tog; Rep once from *; Rep * to **, hdc2tog in next hcd2tog and next hdc, hdc in last 17 hdc, join with sl st in first hdc, turn.

Rnd 21: Ch 1, hdc in first 18 sts, fpdc around each of next 2 bpdc, hdc in next hdc, *hdc2tog in next hdc and top of next bpdc, sk next bpdc, fptr around each of next 2 bpdc, working behind 2 sts just made work fptr around bpdc used in hdc2tog, fptr around sk bpdc, hdc2tog in same st as fptr of cross and next hdc; Rep once from *, hdc in next hdc, fpdc around each of next 2 bpdc, hdc2tog in same st as fpdc just made and next hdc2tog, hdc in last 51 hdc, join with sl st in first hdc, turn.

Rnd 22: Ch 1, hdc in first 53 sts, bpdc around same st as prev hdc, bpdc2tog over next fpdc and next fptr *(skip 2 sts between, see Special Stitches on page 15)*, bpdc around next fptr, 2 hdc in top of same fptr as bpdc just made, hdc in next fptr, bpdc around same fptr as hdc just made, bpdc around next fptr, sk 2 sts, bpdc around each of next 2 fptr, hdc in same st as bpdc just made, 2 hdc in next fptr, bpdc around same fptr as 2 hdc just made, bpdc2tog over next fptr and next fpdc *(skip 2 sts between)*, bpdc around next fpdc, hdc in same st as bpdc just made, hdc in last 18 hdc, join with sl st in first hdc, turn.

Rnd 23: Ch 1, hdc in first 20 sts, *fpdc2tog over same bpdc as hdc just made and next bpdc *(skip bpdc2tog between, see Special Stitches on page 15)*, hdc in second bpdc used for fpdc2tog**, hdc in next 2 hdc, hdc2tog in next hdc and next bpdc, sk 1 bpdc, fptr around each of next 2 bpdc,

working in front of 2 sts just made, work fptr around bpdc used in hdc2tog, fptr around sk bpdc, hdc2tog in same st as second fptr of cross and next hdc, hdc in next 3 sts; Rep * to **, hdc in last 53 hdc, join with sl st in first hdc, turn.

Rnd 24: Ch 1, hdc in first 57 sts, hdc2tog, bpdc around each of next 2 fptr, hdc in same st as bpdc just made, hdc in next fptr, bpdc around same st as hdc just made, bpdc around next fptr, hdc2tog, hdc in last 23 sts, join with sl st in first hdc, turn.

Rnd 25: Ch 1, hdc in first 24 sts, fpdc around each of next 2 bpdc, hdc in next 2 hdc, fpdc around each of next 2 bpdc, hdc2tog in same st as st just made and next hdc2tog, hdc in last 57 hdc, join with sl st in first hdc, turn.

Rnd 26: Ch 1, hdc in first 59 sts, bpdc around same fpdc as hdc just made, bpdc2tog over next 2 fpdc *(skip 2 sts between)*, bpdc around next fpdc, 2 hdc in top of same st as bpdc just made, hdc in last 24 hdc, join with sl st in first hdc, turn.

Rnd 27: Ch 1, hdc in first 27 sts, fpdc2tog over same bpdc as hdc just made and next bpdc *(skip bpdc2tog between)*, hdc in second bpdc used for fpdc2tog, hdc in last 59 hdc, join with sl st in first hdc, turn.

Rnd 28: Ch 1, hdc in each st around, join with sl st in first hdc, turn.

Rnd 29: Ch 1, [sc2tog, sc in next 42 hdc] 2 times, join with sl st in first sc2tog. Finish off and weave in ends. (86 sc)

MITTS PATTERN
(Work stitch counts in parenthesis for Second Mitt, see Pattern Notes.)

Ch 30, careful not to twist, join with sl st in first ch to form ring.

Rnd 1 (RS): Ch 1, sc in the back bump of same ch as join and each ch around, join with sl st in first sc, turn. (30 sc) *(See Tutorials on page 58 or 64 for Back Bump.)*

Rnds 2-6: Ch 1, hdc in each st around, join with sl st in first hdc, turn. (30 hdc)

(Refer to Knotwork Panel diagram on page 19, beginning at Row 3 of diagram.)

Note: Some of the stitches just before and after the cable are different from diagram to fit on Mitts, however, post stitches remain the same. Refer to written pattern as well.

Rnd 7: Ch 1, hdc in first 5(14) hdc, hdc2tog, sk next hdc, fptr around next hdc; Working behind fptr just made hdc in sk hdc, hdc in same hdc as prev fptr, fpdc around same hdc as prev fptr, hdc2tog, hdc in last 19(10) hdc, join with sl st in first hdc, turn. *(See Tutorials on page 60 or 66 for Beginning an Eternal Knot Cable.)*

Rnd 8: Ch 1, hdc in first 18(9) hdc, hdc2tog, bpdc around next fpdc, bpdc around next hdc, hdc in same hdc as bpdc just made, hdc in next hdc, bptr around same hdc as prev bpdc, bpdc around next fptr, hdc2tog, hdc in last 4(13) hdc, join with sl st in first hdc, turn.

Rnd 9: Ch 1, hdc in first 5(14) sts, fpdc around each of next 2 sts, hdc in next 2 hdc, fpdc around each of next 2 sts, hdc2tog in top of same st as fpdc just made and next hdc, hdc in last 18(9) hdc, join with sl st in first hdc, turn.

Rnd 10: Ch 1, hdc in first 20(11) sts, bpdc around same fpdc as hdc just made, bpdc around next fpdc, sk 2 hdc, bpdc around each of next 2 fpdc, hdc in top of same st as st just made, hdc in last 5(14) hdc, join with sl st in first hdc, turn.

Rnd 11: Ch 1, hdc in first sl st, hdc in next 1(10) hdc, *sk next hdc, fptr around next hdc; Working **behind** fptr just made, hdc in sk hdc, hdc in same hdc as prev fptr, fpdc around same hdc as fptr, hdc2tog**, hdc2tog in next hdc and top of first bpdc, sk next bpdc, fptr around each of next 2 bpdc; Working in **front** of 2 sts just made, fptr around bpdc used in hdc2tog, fptr around sk bpdc *(first cross completed)*, hdc2tog in same st as second fptr of cross and next hdc, hdc2tog; Rep * to **, hdc in last 13(4) hdc, join with sl st in first hdc, turn. (32 sts) *(See Tutorials on page 61 or 67.)*

36

Rnd 12: Ch 1, hdc in first sl st, hdc in next 12(3) hdc, hdc2tog, *bpdc around next fpdc, bpdc around next hdc, hdc in same hdc as st just made, hdc in next hdc, bptr around same hdc as prev bpdc, bpdc around next fptr**, sk 2 hdc2tog, bpdc around each of next 2 fptr, hdc in top of same fptr as st just made, hdc in next fptr, bpdc around same fptr as st just made, bpdc around next fptr, sk 2 hdc2tog; Rep * to **, hdc2tog in same st as bpdc just made and next hdc, hdc in last 1(10) hdc, join with sl st in first hdc, turn. (34 sts)

Rnd 13: Ch 1, hdc in first 2(11) sts, fpdc around each of next 2 sts, hdc in next hdc, *hdc2tog in next hdc and top of next bpdc, sk next bpdc, fptr around each of next 2 sts; Working behind 2 sts just made, fptr around bpdc used in hdc2tog, fptr around sk bpdc, hdc2tog in same st as second fptr of cross and next hdc; Rep once from *, hdc in next hdc, fpdc around each of next 2 bpdc, hdc2tog in same st as fpdc just made and next hdc, hdc in next 10(1) hdc, leave last 3 hdc unworked, **do not join**, turn. (31 sts) (*Work in unjoined rnds through Rnd 17.*)

Rnd 14: Ch 1, 2(1) hdc in first hdc, hdc in next 11(2) sts, *bpdc around same post st as hdc just made, bpdc around next post st, sk 2 sts, bpdc around each of next 2 post sts, hdc in top of same post st as bpdc just made**, hdc in next fptr; Rep once from *; Rep once from * to **, hdc in next 1(10) hdc, 1(2) hdc in last hdc, turn. (32 sts)

Rnd 15: Ch 1, 1(2) hdc in first hdc, hdc in next 1(11) hdc, *hdc2tog in next hdc and top of next bpdc, sk next bpdc, fptr around each of next 2 bpdc; Working in front of prev 2 sts, fptr around bpdc used in hdc2tog, fptr around sk bpdc, hdc2tog in same st as second fptr of cross and next

hdc; Rep from * 2 more times, hdc in next 11(1) hdc, 2(1) hdc in last hdc, turn. (33 sts)

Rnd 16: Ch 1, 2(1) hdc in first hdc, hdc in next 11(0) hdc, hdc2tog in next hdc and next hdc2tog, *bpdc around each of next 2 fptr, hdc in same fptr as st just made, hdc in next fptr, bpdc around same fptr as hdc just made, bpdc around next fptr**, sk 2 hdc2tog; Rep once from *; Rep * to **, hdc2tog in same st as prev bpdc and next hcd2tog, hdc in next 1(12) hdc, 1(2) hdc in last hdc, turn. (35 sts)

Rnd 17: Ch 1, 2 hdc in first hdc, hdc in next 2(12) sts, fpdc around each of next 2 bpdc, hdc in next hdc, *hdc2tog in next hdc and top of next bpdc, sk next bpdc, fptr around each of next 2 bpdc, working behind 2 sts just made, work fptr around bpdc used in hdc2tog, fptr around sk bpdc, hdc2tog in same st as second fptr of cross and next hdc; Rep once from *, hdc in next hdc, fpdc around each of next 2 bpdc, hdc2tog in same st as fpdc just made and next hdc2tog, hdc in next 12(2) sts, 2 hdc in last hdc, turn. (37 sts)

Rnd 18: Ch 1, 2 hdc in first hdc, hdc in next 15(4) sts, bpdc around same st as hdc just made, bpdc2tog over next fpdc and next fptr (*skip 2 sts between, see Special Stitches*), bpdc around next fptr, 2 hdc in top of same fptr as bpdc just made, hdc in next fptr, bpdc around same fptr as hdc just made, bpdc around next fptr, sk 2 hdc2tog, bpdc around each of next 2 fptr, hdc in same st as bpdc just made, 2 hdc in next fptr, bpdc around same fptr as 2 hdc just made, bpdc2tog over next fptr and next fpdc (*skip 2 sts between*), bpdc around next fpdc, hdc in same st as bpdc just made, hdc in next 3(14) hdc, 2 hdc in last hdc, join with sl st in first hdc, turn. (39 sts)

Rnd 19: Ch 1, hdc2tog 2 times, hdc in next 3(14) sts, *fpdc2tog over same bpdc as hdc just made and next bpdc *(skip bpdc2tog between, see Special Stitches)*, hdc in second bpdc used for fpdc2tog**, hdc in next 2 hdc, hdc2tog in next hdc and next bpdc, sk 1 bpdc, fptr around each of next 2 bpdc, working in front of prev 2 sts work fptr around bpdc used in hdc2tog, fptr around sk bpdc, hdc2tog in same st as second fptr of cross and next hdc, hdc in next 3 sts; Rep * to **, hdc in next 15(4) hdc, hdc2tog, join with sl st in first hdc, turn. (36 sts)

Rnd 20: Ch 1, hdc2tog, hdc in next 18(7) sts, hdc2tog, bpdc around each of next 2 fptr, hdc in same st as bpdc just made, hdc in next fptr, bpdc around same st as hdc just made, bpdc around next fptr, hdc2tog, hdc in next 6(17) hdc, hdc2tog, join with sl st in first hdc, turn. (34 sts)

Rnd 21: Ch 1, hdc2tog, hdc in next 6(17) sts, fpdc around each of next 2 bpdc, hdc in next 2 hdc, fpdc around each of next 2 bpdc, hdc2tog in same st as st just made and next hdc2tog, hdc in next 17(6) hdc, hdc2tog, join with sl st in first hdc, turn. (32 sts)

Rnd 22: Ch 1, hdc2tog, hdc in next 18(7) sts, bpdc around same fpdc as hdc just made, bpdc2tog over next 2 fpdc *(skip 2 sts between)*, bpdc around next fpdc, 2 hdc in top of same st as bpdc just made, hdc in next 5(16) hdc, hdc2tog, join with sl st in first hdc, turn. (30 sts)

Rnd 23: Ch 1, hdc in first 10(20) sts, fpdc2tog over same bpdc as hdc just made and next bpdc *(skip bpdc2tog between)*, hdc in second bpdc used for fpdc2tog, hdc in last 18(8) hdc, join with sl st in first hdc, turn.

Rnds 24-28: Rep Rnd 2.

Rnd 29: Ch 1, sc in each hdc around, join with sl st in first sc. Fasten off.

Thumb (repeat on both Mitts)
Join with sl st in last st used on Rnd 13 before 3 skipped sts.

Rnd 1: Ch 1, work 20 hdc evenly around thumbhole, join with sl st in first hdc, turn (20 hdc)

Rnd 2: Ch 1, [hdc2tog, hdc in next 5 hdc] 2 times, hdc2tog, hdc in next 4 hdc, join with sl st in first hdc2tog, turn. (17 hdc)

Rnd 3: Ch 1, hdc2tog, hdc in next 15 hdc, join with sl st in first hdc2tog, turn. (16 hdc)

Rnds 4-5: Ch 1, hdc in each hdc around, join with sl st in first hdc, turn.

Rnd 6: Ch 1, hdc in first 14 hdc, hdc2tog, join with sl st in first hdc, turn. (15 hdc)

Rnd 7: Ch 1, sc2tog, sc in each hdc around, join with sl st in first sc2tog. Finish off. (14 sc)

Mrs. Donaghue's Cape

Grahame surprised me at the bottom of the stairs with a cape. It was wool the same creamy color as his sheep. It was thick and warm and all it lacked was a hood to complete it. He held it out like an offering.

I ran my fingers over it. The wool was scratchy but dry and thick.

I looked up at him, and my question must have been plain on my face.

"I bought it in town," he said.

"While I was still on the ship?"

"I thought you might have need of it."

It was the closest thing to a whim I'd seen in him. It was a lovely cape, and completely useless on a farm. It was too long and too round and would have been nothing but in my way as I worked. But for a walk, it was perfect. And I loved it.

Alternated stitches of single and double crochet create a thick wool cape, inspired by the one Grahame gifts to his new wife. Worked in undyed Highland Wool as Ailee would have spun it, right off the sheep.

Difficulty
Advance Beginner

Finished Size
41"(104cm) long
42"(107cm) around shoulder
56"(142cm) around bottom edge

Yarn
Approx. 1800yds(1646m)/ 32oz(907g) heavy worsted weight yarn.

Yarn used for sample: Cascade Ecological Wool, 100% Peruvian Wool (250g/8.75oz, 478yds/ 437m), 4 skeins in Natural

Notions
- Size J/6.0mm crochet hook, or hook to get gauge
- Three 7/8"(2 ¼cm) - 1"(2 ½ cm) wooden buttons from Craftwich Creations
- Stitch Markers
- Tapestry Needle

Gauge
11 sts by 10 rows = 4"(10cm) in [dc, sc] pattern stitch

PATTERN NOTES

- Beginning chain does not count as first dc or hdc throughout. Instead, chain 1 and pull up to height of next stitch worked into first stitch.
- Standing stitches are used to join yarn at the height of the stitches on the row, eliminating the need for a chain to get to the correct height. See Special Stitches and Tutorials in back of book.
- Button placement can be adjusted to fit shoulders.

SPECIAL STITCHES *(See Tutorials on page 59 or 65 for Standing Stitches)*

Standing Single Crochet (standing sc): With slip knot on hook, insert hook into indicated stitch, yo, pull up loop, yo, pull through 2 loops on hook.

Standing Half Double Crochet (standing hdc): With slip knot on hook, yo, insert hook into indicated stitch, yo, pull up loop, yo, pull through all 3 loops on hook.

Standing Double Crochet (standing dc): With slip knot on hook, yo, insert hook into indicated stitch, yo, pull up loop, [yo, pull through 2 loops on hook] 2 times.

Tip for Working Standing Stitches – Hold slip knot on hook with index finger to avoid it spinning on hook when you start a standing stitch.

CAPE PATTERN

SHOULDERS

Chain 48.

Row 1: Sc in second ch from hook and each ch across, turn – 47 sts.

Row 2: Ch 1, dc in first sc, [sc in next sc, dc in next sc] 2 times, *(sc, dc, sc) in next sc, [dc in next sc, sc in next sc] 5 times, dc in next sc; Rep from * 2 more times, (sc, dc, sc) in next sc, [dc in next sc, sc in next sc] 2 times, dc in last sc, turn. (55 sts)

Row 3: Ch 1, sc in first dc, dc in next sc, [sc in next dc, dc in next sc] 2 times, *(sc, dc, sc) in next dc, [dc in next sc, sc in next dc] 6 times, dc in next sc; Rep from * 2 more times, (sc, dc, sc) in next dc, [dc in next sc, sc in next dc] 3 times, turn. (63 sts)

Row 4: Ch 1, dc in first sc, [sc in next dc, dc in next sc] 3 times, *(sc, dc, sc) in next dc, [dc in next sc, sc in next dc] 7 times, dc in next sc; Rep from * 2 more times, (sc, dc, sc) in next dc, [dc in next sc, sc in next dc] 3 times, dc in last sc, turn. (71 sts)

Row 5: Ch 1, sc in first dc, dc in next sc, [sc in next dc, dc in next sc] 3 times, *(sc, dc, sc) in next dc, [dc in next sc, sc in next dc] 8 times, dc in next sc; Rep from * 2 more times, (sc, dc, sc) in next dc, [dc in next sc, sc in next dc] 4 times, turn. (79 sts)

Row 6: Ch 1, dc in first sc, [sc in next dc, dc in next sc] 4 times, *(sc, dc, sc) in next dc, [dc in next sc, sc in next dc] 9 times, dc in next sc; Rep from * 2 more times, (sc, dc, sc) in next dc, [dc in next sc, sc in next dc] 4 times, dc in last sc, turn. (87 sts)

Row 7: Ch 1, sc in first dc, dc in next sc, [sc in next dc, dc in next sc] 4 times, *(sc, dc, sc) in next dc, [dc in next sc, sc in next dc] 10 times, dc in next sc; Rep from * 2 more times, (sc, dc, sc) in next dc, [dc in next sc, sc in next dc] 5 times, turn. (95 sts)

Row 8: Ch 1, dc in first sc, [sc in next dc, dc in next sc] 5 times, *(sc, dc, sc) in next dc, [dc in next sc, sc in next dc] 11 times, dc in next sc; Rep from * 2 more times, (sc, dc, sc) in next dc, [dc in next sc, sc in next dc] 5 times, dc in last sc, turn. (103 sts)

Row 9: Ch 1, sc in first dc, dc in next sc, [sc in next dc, dc in next sc] 5 times, *(sc, dc, sc) in next dc, [dc in next sc, sc in next dc] 12 times, dc in next sc; Rep from * 2 more times, (sc, dc, sc) in next dc, [dc in next sc, sc in next dc] 6 times, turn. (111 sts)

Row 10: Ch 1, dc in first sc, [sc in next dc, dc in next sc] 6 times, *(sc, dc, sc) in next dc, [dc in next sc, sc in next dc] 13 times, dc in next sc; Rep from * 2 more times, (sc, dc, sc) in next dc, [dc in next sc, sc in next dc] 6 times, dc in last sc, turn. (119 sts)

Row 11: Ch 1, sc in first dc, [dc in next sc, sc in next dc] across, turn.

Row 12: Ch 1, dc in first sc, sc in next dc, [dc in next sc, sc in next dc] 6 times, *(dc, sc, dc) in next sc, [sc in next dc, dc in next sc] 14 times, sc in next dc; Rep from * 2 more times, (dc, sc, dc) in next sc, [sc in next dc, dc in next sc] 7 times, turn. (127 sts)

Row 13: Repeat Row 11.

Row 14: Ch 1, dc in first sc, [sc in next dc, dc in next sc] 7 times, *(sc, dc, sc) in next dc, [dc in next sc, sc in next dc] 15 times, dc in next sc; Rep from * 2 more times, (sc, dc, sc) in next dc, [dc in next sc, sc in next dc] 7 times, dc in next sc, turn. (135 sts)

Row 15: Repeat Row 11.

Row 16: Ch 1, dc in first sc, sc in next dc, [dc in next sc, sc in next dc] 7 times, *(dc, sc, dc) in next sc, [sc in next dc, dc in next sc] 16 times, sc in next dc; Rep from * 2 more times, (dc, sc, dc) in next sc, [sc in next dc, dc in next sc] 8 times, turn. (143 sts)

Row 17: Repeat Row 11.

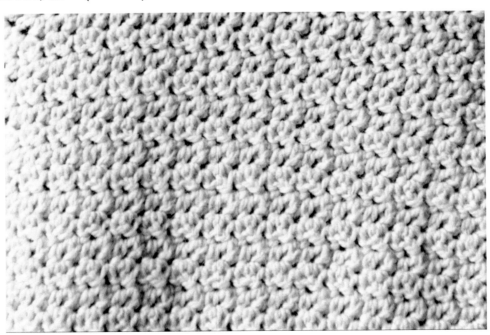

43

Row 18: Ch 1, dc in first sc, [sc in next dc, dc in next sc] across, turn.

Row 19: Ch 1, sc in first dc, [dc in next sc, sc in next dc] 8 times, *(dc, sc, dc) in next sc, [sc in next dc, dc in next sc] 17 times, sc in next dc; Rep from * 2 more times, (dc, sc, dc) in next sc, [sc in next dc, dc in next sc] 8 times, sc in next dc, turn. (151 sts)

Rows 20-22: Alternate Rows 18 and 11.

Row 23: Ch 1, sc in first dc, dc in next sc, [sc in next dc, dc in next sc] 8 times, *(sc, dc, sc) in next sc, [dc in next sc, sc in next dc] 18 times, dc in next sc; Rep from * 2 more times, (sc, dc, sc) in next sc, [dc in next sc, sc in next dc] 9 times, turn. (159 sts)

Rows 24-36: Alternate Rows 18 and 11, ending with Row 18. Do not finish off.

ARMHOLES
Place Stitch Markers in 25th stitch and 136th stitch to mark where Back and Second Front will start.

First Front
Continued from Row 36 of Shoulders.

Row 1: Ch 1, [sc in next dc, dc in next sc] 12 times, leave remaining stitches unworked, turn. (24 sts)

Rows 2-15: Repeat Row 1. Finish off.

Back
Join with standing sc *(see Special Stitches)* in first stitch with stitch marker.

Row 1: [Dc in next sc, sc in next dc] 55 times, leave remaining stitches unworked, turn. (111 sts)

Row 2: Ch 1, dc in first sc, [sc in next dc, dc in next sc] 55 times, turn.

Row 3: Ch 1, sc in first dc, [dc in next sc, sc in next dc] 55 times, turn.

Rows 4-15: Alternate Rows 2 and 3. Finish off.

Second Front
Join with standing dc *(see Special Stitches)* in second stitch with stitch marker.

Row 1: Sc in next dc, [dc in next sc, sc in next dc] 11 times, turn. (24 sts)

Row 2: Ch 1, [dc in next sc, sc in next dc] 12 times, turn.

Rows 3-15: Repeat row 2. Do not finish off.

LOWER SECTION
Continued from Row 15 of Second Front. Rejoin the Fronts to the Back by working continuous stitches.

Row 1: Ch 1, [dc in next sc, sc in next dc] 12 times, skip over first armhole, dc in first sc of Back, [sc in next dc, dc in next sc] 55 times, skip over second armhole, sc in first dc of First Front, dc in next sc, [sc in next dc, dc in next sc] 11 times, turn. (159 sts)

Row 2: Ch 1, sc in first dc, [dc in next sc, sc in next dc] across, turn.

Row 3: Ch 1, dc in first sc, [sc in next dc, dc in next sc] across, turn.

Rows 4-53: Alternate Rows 2 and 3. Finish off.

COLLAR

First-Side Collar
Work along neckline in unused loops of beg chain of Cape. With WS facing, join with standing hdc in unused loops of first chain (on right-side for right-handed or left-side for left-handed crocheters).

Row 1: Hdc in same st as join, hdc in next 6 st, 2 hdc in next st, hdc in next 7 sts, 2 hdc in next st, hdc in next 6 sts, 2 hdc in next hdc, leave remaining sts unworked, turn. (27 hdc)

Row 2: Ch 1, 2 hdc in first hdc, hdc in next 4 hdc, [2 hdc in next hdc, hdc in next 3 hdc] 5 times, hdc in next hdc, 2 hdc in last hdc, turn. (34 hdc)

Row 3: Ch 1, 2 hdc in first hdc, [hdc in first 10 hdc, 2 hdc in next hdc] 3 times, turn. (38 hdc)

Row 4: Ch 1, hdc in first 37 hdc, 2 hdc in last hdc, turn. (39 hdc)

Row 5: Ch 1, hdc2tog in first 2 hdc, hdc in each hdc across to last 2 hdc, hdc2tog, turn. (37 hdc)

Row 6: Ch 1, hdc2tog in first 2 hdc, hdc in next 32 hdc, hdc2tog, leave last hdc2tog unworked. Finish off. (34 hdc)

Second-Side Collar
With WS facing, sk next st left unworked from First-Side, join with standing hdc in unused loops of next st. Repeat Rows 1-6 of First Side.

FINISHING

Cape Edging

With RS facing, join with standing sc in last st of Row 53 of Lower Section.

Rnd 1: Sc in each st across to last sc of bottom edge, 3 sc in corner st, sc evenly across first side *(approx. 5 sts in sides of every 4 rows)*, sc evenly around first Collar, sl st in sk st between Collars, sc evenly around second Collar; Sc in first st of second

side, ch 7, sc in same st as prev sc *(first buttonhole formed)*, [18 sc worked evenly in sides of next 14 rows, ch 7, sc in same st as prev sc] 2 times, sc evenly down rest of side, 2 sc in same st as first sc, join with sl st in first sc, turn.

Row 2: Ch 1, sl st in each sc around, join with sl st in first sl st, turn. Finish off.

Armhole Edging (work same for each Armhole)
With RS facing, join with sl st in bottom join of armhole, work 22 sc evenly up first side, sl st in top join of armhole, work 22 sc evenly down second side, join with sl st in first sl st. (46 sts)

Buttons
Use leftover yarn and a tapestry needle to sew buttons onto side without button holes, 1 to 2 inches from the edge, adjusting for fit around shoulders. *Tip: Tie buttons in place and try on to allow for adjustments before they are sewn on.*

Blocking
Steam block finished cape to smooth fabric and add drape.

Alternative Design Ideas

- Make a Shorter Capelet by ending before the armholes.
- Skip the collar for a simpler cape.
- Use ties instead of buttonholes by chaining to desired length then slip stitching back into the chains.

Niall watched me warily as I approached.

"I want you to have this," I told him, holding out the cowl I'd finished earlier in the week. I'd treated it with wool oil already.

Niall looked surprised. "Why?"

"To keep you safe."

He looked dubious, but I was prepared for that. "I know you don't believe me about the beast. You don't have to. But I do wish you might wear this anyway if you go into the woods. At least when it's cool outside."

Niall took the cowl, turning it over in his hands. "It's finely made," he conceded.

Difficulty
Advance Beginner

Finished Size
Pattern for 2 sizes using 1 or 2 skeins. 60"/152 ½cm circumference, 7"/18cm (11"/28cm) deep

Yarn
140yds/128m (220yds/ 201m) Super Bulky Weight Yarn. Samples shown used Dredz from Abstract Fiber, 1 (2) skeins in Cascade (140yds/128m, 8.8oz/250g)

Notions
- Size Q/15mm crochet hook or hook to get gauge
- Yarn Needle
- Stitch Marker

Gauge
6 sts by 8 rows sc = 4"(10cm)

A cozy cowl worked on a large hook, alternates front and back loop only single crochets for a luscious texture that whips up in a flash.

PATTERN NOTES

- Instructions for larger size in parenthesis( ).
- Worked in continuous rounds, both sides of the fabric look a little different but good.

SPECIAL STITCHES

Front Loop Only Single Crochet (floSC): Insert hook under front loop of next single crochet, yo, pull up a loop, yo, pull through 2 loops.

Back Loop Only Single Crochet (bloSC): Insert hook under back loop of next single crochet, yo, pull up a loop, yo, pull through 2 loops.

COWL PATTERN

Ch 75, careful not to twist, join with sl st in first ch to form large ring.

Rnd 1: Sc in back bump *(see Tutorials on page 58 or 64)* of each ch around, join with sl st in first sc. (75 sc) Worked in continuous rounds from here, place a stitch marker in first sc and move up at end of each rnd.

Rnd 2: BloSC in first sc, [floSC in next sc, bloSC in next sc] around, do not join.

Rnd 3: Ch 1, floSC in first sc, [bloSC in next sc, floSC in next sc] around.

Rnds 4 - 10(16): Alternate Rnds 2 and 3, ending with Rnd 2. Finish off and weave in ends.

MARJORIE'S WRAPPED SHAWL

Of the townsfolk, they were dressed differently as well, in thick clothing suited to the climate and oddly shaped hats. The aprons and shawls the women wore were of a different cut than I was used to, the shawls wrapping round the women's torsos to tie in back.

Inspired by the wrap shawls commonly worn in the time period of our story, slip stitch crochet worked in the front loop only gives the stretchy ribbed look of knit with the ease of using a hook.

Difficulty
Advance Beginner

Finished Size
59"/150cm(69"/175cm) wingspan, 24"/61cm(30 ½"/ 77 ½cm) long, plus 10"(25½cm) ties

Yarn
Approx. 900yds/823m heavy worsted weight yarn

Yarn used for sample: Cascade Ecological Wool (250g/8.75oz, 478yds/ 437m), 2 skeins in Chocolate Brown

Notions
N/10mm crochet hook, adjust to get gauge
Scissors, Stitch Markers, Tapestry Needle

Gauge
8 sts by 9 rows in floSlSt = 2"/5cm

PATTERN NOTES

- Instructions for larger size in parenthesis( ).
- Worked from one end to the other gradually increasing and decreasing.

SPECIAL STITCHES

Front Loop Only Slip Stitch (floSlSt): Insert hook into front loop only of next st, yo, pull loop through st and first loop on hook.

Picot (pic): Ch 3, sl st in third ch from hook.

SHAWL PATTERN

Ch 5. Work in front loop only throughout. *(See Tutorials on page 62 or 68 for SlSts.)*

Row 1: Sl st in second ch from hook and each ch across, turn. (4 sl st)

Rows 2-3: Ch 1, floSlSt *(see Special Stitches)* in beg ch and each sl st across, turn. (6 sl st)

Rows 4-30: Ch 1, floSlSt in each sl st across.

Row 31: Ch 1, floSlSt in beg ch and each sl st across, turn. (7 sl st)

Rows 32-34: Ch 1, floSlSt in each sl st across.

Rows 35-50: Rep Rows 31-34 four more times. (11 sl st)

Rows 51-53: Ch 1, floSlSt in beg ch and each sl st across, turn. (14 sl st)

Row 54: Ch 1, floSlSt in each sl st across.

Rows 55-98: Rep Rows 51-54 eleven more times. (47 sl st)

Row 99: Ch 1, floSlSt in beg ch and each sl st across, turn. (48 sl st)

Row 100: Ch 1, floSlSt in each sl st across.

Rows 101-180 (101- 204): Rep Rows 99 and 100 forty (fifty-two) more times. (88 (100) sl st)

Row 181 (205): Ch 1, sk first sl st, floSlSt in each remaining sl st, turn. – 87 (99) sl st

Row 182 (206): Ch 1, floSlSt in each sl st across.

Rows 183-262 (207-310): Rep Rows 181 (205) and 182 (206) forty(fifty-two) more times. (47 sl st)

Rows 263-265 (311-313): Ch 1, sk first sl st, floSlSt in each remaining sl st, turn. (44 sl st)

Row 266 (314): Ch 1, floSlSt in each sl st across.

Rows 267-310 (315-358): Rep Rows 263-266(311-314) eleven more times. (11 sl st)

Row 311 (359): Ch 1, sk first sl st, floSlSt in each remaining sl st, turn. (10 sl st)

Rows 312-314 (360-362): Ch 1, floSlSt in each sl st across.

Rows 315-326 (363-374): Rep Rows 311-314(359-362) three more times. (7 sl st)

Row 327 (375): Ch 1, sk first sl st, floSlSt in each remaining sl st, turn. (6 sl st)

Rows 328-356 (376-404): Ch 1, floSlSt in each sl st across.

Rows 357-358 (405-406): Ch 1, sk first sl st, floSlSt in each remaining sl st, turn. Do not finish off. (4 sl st)

Edging
Working in both loops of last row and under beg ch 1 of each row down sides of Shawl.

Rnd 1: Ch 1, 2 sc in first sl st, sc in next 2 sl sts, 2 sc in last sl st, turn to work down first side, *sc in side of first row of sl st; working under beg ch 1 of each row, 1 sc in side of every 2 rows of sl st** across to point of corner, 3 sc in corner point of shawl, continue 1 sc in side of every 2 rows of sl st to other end; Working in unused loops of beg ch, 2 sc in first ch, sc in next 2 ch, 2 sc in last ch; Rep * to ** down collar side, join with sl st in first sc, turn.

Rnd 2: Ch 1, sl st in first 21 sc, sk 2 sc, (4 dc, picot *(see Special Stitches)*, 4 dc) in next sc, sk 2 sc, [(4 dc, picot, 4 dc) in next sc, sk 2 sc, sc in next sc, sk 2 sc] 22(26) times, sl st in each remaining st around, join with sl st in first sl st. Finish off and weave in ends.

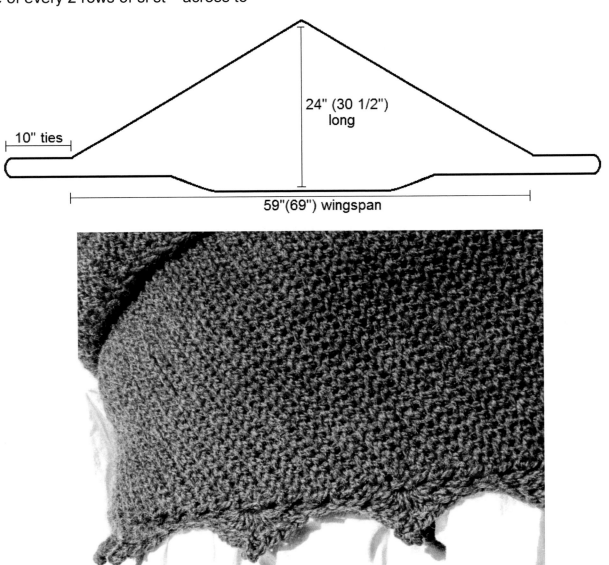

10" ties

24" (30 1/2") long

59"(69") wingspan

53

GRAHAME'S GORGET

I recalled the way the armor seemed to flow from head to neck to shoulders, like a mantle or a monk's cowl, but close, protective. Thick.

And an image began to form in my head about that sort of thing in wool. I'd want something that would fit close to Grahame's neck but also cover his shoulders, so it would need to be wide at the bottom and grow narrow to fit close under the chin. It wouldn't be all one piece, like the cowl, but open at the ends so that Grahame could wear it as tight or loose as he wished. But how to close it? A bit of rope, perhaps, worked through the stitches? Twine? Leather?

Leather would hold best. Maybe with a buckle, like from a harness. Did we have any harnesses left?

A cozy, snug fitting cowl designed to be worn open at the shoulder or front. Top of side edges can be held together with a clasp or button, or seamed closed, and still stretch easily over the head. Luscious super bulky yarn worked in a dense stitch provides warm protection from winter's chill while a large hook creates a deceptively light weight fabric.

Difficulty
Intermediate

Finished Size
Width: 22"(56cm) neck, 36"(91 ½cm) shoulders
Length: 7 ½"(19cm) center, 11 ½"(29cm) at sides

Yarn Used
140yds(128m) Super Bulky Weight Yarn

Yarn used for samples Dredz from Abstract Fiber, 1 skein in Mousse and Cascade (140yds/128m, 8.8oz/250g)

Notions
- Size P/15mm crochet hook or hook to get gauge (*see Pattern Notes*)
- Yarn Needle
- 2 Small leather belts or closures (Craftwich Creations)

Gauge
6 sts by 8 rows in lb-sc = 4"(10cm)

PATTERN NOTES

- **Important Note on Hook Shape:** P hooks come in a variety of shapes and sizes, ranging from 10mm-15mm. Choose an "in-line" shaped hook like Craftwich Creations (shown in tutorials) or Susan Bates©. Hooks with a smaller head than the rest of the hook can make your gauge much smaller.
- "Lower bar" stitches create a dense fabric by avoiding holes formed when working with a large hook and thick yarn.
- When increasing over short rows (beginning with Row 17) working "sc in side of slst 2 rows down" creates a more continuous, smooth fabric. If part of stitch is still visible, disrupting the smooth fabric, try stitch again inserting under those loops.

SPECIAL STITCHES *(See Tutorials on pages 63 and 69)*

Lower Bar Single Crochet (lb-sc): Insert hook under 3 loops of next single crochet with hook coming out back of stitch through center of single crochet stitch, yo, pull up a loop, yo, pull through 2 loops.

Lower Bar Slip Stitch (lb-slst): Insert hook under 3 loops of next single crochet with hook coming out back of stitch through center of single crochet stitch, yo, pull loop through stitch and first loop on hook.

COWL PATTERN

Ch 17.

Row 1: Sc in back bump *(see Tutorials on page 58 or 64)* of second ch from hook and each ch across, turn. (16 sc)

Row 2: Ch 1, lb-sc in each sc across to last sc, lb-slst in last st, turn. (15 sc)

Row 3: Ch 1, sk slst, lb-sc in each sc across, turn.

Row 4: Ch 1, lb-sc in each sc across, slst in turning ch, turn.

Row 5: Ch 1, sk slst, lb-sc in each sc across, turn.

Rows 6-9: Rep Rows 2-5. (14 sc)

Row 10: Ch 1, lb-sc in each sc across to last sc, lb-slst in last st, turn. (13 sc)

Begin Short Rows

Row 11: Ch 1, sk slst, lb-sc in next 9 sc, lb-slst in next sc, leave 3 sc unworked, turn. (9 sc)

Row 12: Ch 1, sk slst, lb-sc in each sc across, turn.

Row 13: Ch 1, lb-sc in next 6 sc, lb-slst in next sc, turn. (6 sc)

Row 14: Ch 1, sk slst, lb-sc in each sc across, turn.

Row 15: Ch 1, lb-sc in next 3 sc, lb-slst in next sc, turn. (3 sc)

Row 16: Ch 1, sk slst, lb-sc in each sc across, turn.

Row 17: Ch 1, lb-sc in next 3 sc, sc in side of slst 2 rows down, lb-sc in next sc, lb-slst in next sc, turn. (5 sc)

Row 18: Ch 1, sk slst, lb-sc in each sc across, turn.

Row 19: Ch 1, lb-sc in next 5 sc, [sc in side of slst 2 rows down] 2 times, lb-sc in next sc, lb-slst in next sc, turn. (8 sc)

Row 20: Ch 1, sk slst, lb-sc in each sc across, turn.

Row 21: Ch 1, lb-sc in next 8 sc, [sc in side of slst 2 rows down] 2 times, lb-sc in last 3 sc, turn. (13 sc)

Rows 22-23: Rep Rows 2-3. (12 sc)

Rows 24-30: Ch 1, lb-sc in each sc across, turn.

Row 31: Ch 1, lb-sc in next 9 sc, lb-slst in next sc, leave 2 sc unworked, turn. (9 sc)

Rows 32-40: Rep Rows 12-20.

Row 41: Ch 1, lb-sc in next 8 sc, [sc in side of slst 2 rows down] 2 times, lb-sc in last 2 sc, turn. (12 sc)

Rows 42-50: Ch 1, lb-sc in each sc across, turn.

Row 51: Ch 1, 2 lb-sc in first sc, lb-sc in next 7 sc, lb-slst in next sc, leave remaining 3 sts unworked, turn. (9 sc)

Rows 52-61: Rep Rows 12-21. (13 sc)

Tips for Working Short Rows
- Short rows allow for shaping by leaving some stitches unworked with gradually fewer stitches, then working back up to the total width of the fabric.
- When increasing the number of stitches in short rows, you will insert hook into sides of slip stitches of previous rows and will work into single crochets more than 1 row below the current row.

Row 62: Ch 1, lb-sc in each sc across, sc in ch 1 at end of prev row, slst in same st as prev sc, turn. (14 sc)

Row 63: Ch 1, lb-sc in each sc across, turn.

Row 64: Ch 1, lb-sc in each sc across, slst in turning ch, turn.

Row 65: Ch 1, sk slst, lb-sc in each sc across, turn.

Row 66: Ch 1, lb-sc in each sc across, sc in side of slst 2 rows down, turn. (15 sc)

Rows 67-70: Rep Rows 63-66. Finish off and weave in ends. (16 sc)

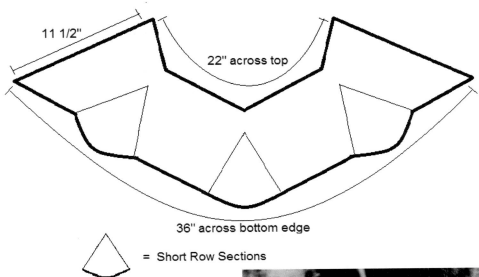

11 1/2"

22" across top

36" across bottom edge

= Short Row Sections

Finishing Options for Cowl
- Use **leather closures** to hold top edges together. Overlap approx. 3 stitches at neck for a snugger fit. In samples shown, top closure is inserted between stitches on 4th row from each side and bottom closure is inserted through 2nd row on each side.
- Sew 1 or 2 **buttons** on one side and create chain loop button holes with remaining yarn on other side.
- Use yarn to **stitch together** top third of stitches along side edges leaving remaining stitches open.

STITCHES FOR GETTING STARTED
Working Into Back Bump of Chain:

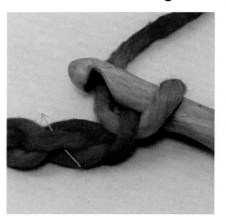 

Reverse Slip Knot (alternative to Magic Loop)

 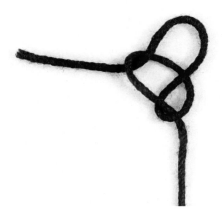 

Form yarn loop in a cursive letter "e".

Reach through and pull up loop with short end of yarn.

Tighten knot with long end. Short end will be adjustable.

Working Into Reverse Slip Knot (or Adjustable Loop)

Chain as indicated. First chain counts as adjustable ring.

When working stitches, insert hook under 2 loops of first ch.

Work all indicated stitches into first chain made.

Pull short end to tighten adjustable ring.

STANDING STITCHES FOR JOINING NEW YARN

Standing Single Crochet:

Begin with a slip knot on your hook. Hold in place with index finger.
Insert hook in first stitch, pull up loop and complete first single crochet

Standing Double Crochet:

Begin with slip knot on hook.
Yo, holding first loop in place
with index finger.

Insert hook in indicated stitch.

Yarn over, pull up loop.

Yarn over, pull through 2 loops.

Yarn over, pull through 2 loops.

59

CABLE STITCHES

Beginning an Eternal Knot Cable:

Following an hdc2tog, sk 1 hdc.

Yo 2 times, insert hook from front around post of next hdc.

Complete first fptr.

Work hdc in skipped stitch and next hdc.

Yo, insert hook around post of same hdc as previous fptr.

Complete fpdc for other side of closed "eternal" knot.

Beginning a Crossed Cable:

Skip first 2 front post stitches.

Yo 2 times, insert hook from front around post of next front post stitch.

Complete first fptr.

Work second fptr around next post stitch.

60

Cable Crossed in Front of Previous Stitches:

Work next fptr around first skipped stitch, keeping hook and yarn in front of sts just made.

Complete first fptr.

Work next fptr around second skipped fptr, inserting in front of prev stitches in same way.

Cable Crossed in Back of Previous Stitches:

Work next fptr around first skipped stitch, inserting hook behind stitches just made.

Fold 2 sts just made forward to access first skipped stitch. Complete first fptr.

Work next fptr around second skipped fptr, inserting behind prev stitches in same way.

Note: All crossed cables in these patterns are worked with right side facing making it easier to see sts.

FRONT LOOP ONLY SLIP STITCH STITCHES

Getting Started:

Chain indicated number. Slip stitch in top loop only of second chain from hook.

Increasing in Front Loop Only Slip Stitch:

Increase at the beginning of floSlSt rows by working the first stitch into to front loop of the turning chain.

WORKING INTO THE "LOWER BAR"

Inserting Hook into "Lower Bar":

Insert hook under 3 loops of indicated stitch for both lb-sc and lb-slst. This includes both normal loops at top of stitch and next loop down (or "lower bar").

Shown from **back side of work**: hook will come out through center of "V" shape at back of the stitch. Stitches will line up in straight lines on both sides of the fabric.

Single Crochet into "Lower Bar":

Insert hook under all three loops.

Completed lb-sc. "V"s stack on top of each other on both sides of the fabric.

STITCHES FOR GETTING STARTED

Working Into Back Bump of Chain:

Reverse Slip Knot (alternative to Magic Loop)

Form yarn loop in a cursive letter "e".	Reach through and pull up loop with short end of yarn.	Tighten knot with long end. Short end will be adjustable.

Working Into Reverse Slip Knot (or Adjustable Loop)

Chain as indicated. First chain counts as adjustable ring.	When working stitches, insert hook under 2 loops of first ch.	Work all indicated stitches into first chain made.	Pull short end to tighten adjustable ring.

STANDING STITCHES FOR JOINING NEW YARN

Standing Single Crochet:

Begin with a slip knot on your hook. Hold in place with index finger.
Insert hook in first stitch, pull up loop and complete first single crochet

Standing Double Crochet:

Begin with slip knot on hook. Yo, holding first loop in place with index finger. | Insert hook in indicated stitch. | Yarn over, pull up loop.

Yarn over, pull through 2 loops.　　　　Yarn over, pull through 2 loops.

CABLE STITCHES

Beginning an Eternal Knot Cable:

Following an hdc2tog, sk 1 hdc.

Yo 2 times, insert hook from front around post of next hdc.

Complete first fptr.

Work hdc in skipped stitch and next hdc.

Yo, insert hook around post of same hdc as previous fptr.

Complete fpdc for other side of closed "eternal" knot.

Beginning a Crossed Cable:

Skip first 2 front post stitches.

Yo 2 times, insert hook from front around post of next front post stitch.

Complete first fptr.

Work second fptr around next post stitch.

66

Cable Crossed in Front of Previous Stitches:

Work next fptr around first skipped stitch, keeping hook and yarn in front of sts just made.

Complete first fptr.

Work next fptr around second skipped fptr, inserting in front of prev stitches in same way.

Cable Crossed in Back of Previous Stitches:

Work next fptr around first skipped stitch, inserting hook behind stitches just made.

Fold 2 sts just made forward to access first skipped stitch. Complete first fptr.

Work next fptr around second skipped fptr, inserting behind prev stitches in same way.

Note: All crossed cables in these patterns are worked with right side facing making it easier to see sts.

FRONT LOOP ONLY SLIP STITCH STITCHES

Getting Started:

Chain indicated number. Slip stitch in top loop only of second chain from hook.

Increasing in Front Loop Only Slip Stitch:

Increase at the beginning of floSlSt rows by working the first stitch into to front loop of the turning chain.

WORKING INTO THE "LOWER BAR"

Inserting Hook into "Lower Bar":

Insert hook under 3 loops of indicated stitch for both lb-sc and lb-slst. This includes both normal loops at top of stitch and next loop down (or "lower bar").

Shown from **back side of work**: hook will come out through center of "V" shape at back of the stitch. Stitches will line up in straight lines on both sides of the fabric.

Single Crochet into "Lower Bar":

Insert hook under all three loops.

Completed lb-sc. "V"s stack on top of each other on both sides of the fabric.

Resources for Materials

Yarn

Abstract Fiber
abstractfiber.com

Alexandra's Crafts
alexandrascrafts.com

Black Trillium Fibres
blacktrilliumfibres.com

Cascade Yarns
cascadeyarns.com

Dragynknyts Fiber and Dye Works
dragynknyts.com

Stitchjones
etsy.com/shop/stitchjones

Hooks and Notions

Craftwich Creations
Hooks and accessories
etsy.com/shop/craftwich

Susan Bates
coatsandclark.com

Other

Ficstitches Yarns Crochet Kit Club
ficstitchesyarns.com

C. Jane Reid
author of the Unraveling fiction series
cjanereid.com

The Unraveling Series

All designs in this book are inspired by *The Secret Stitch,* the first book in a new fiber fiction series, *Unraveling*, by C. Jane Reid. The series traces the evolution of crochet against the backdrop of the developing New World. Featuring strong women, historical detail, and a crochet pattern by Laurinda Reddig, each story brings readers one step closer to solving an ancient mystery.

Ficstitches Yarns Crochet Kit Club

Several of the patterns in this book were first published as part of Ficstitches Yarns, a quarterly kit club that takes creating to another level by offering crochet patterns along with hand-dyed yarn, handmade accessories and hooks, and fictional stories, all bound together in a theme of romance, history, the coming-together of friends, and a touch of magic. So much more than a yarn club, each element of these kits is an adventure, with a little bit of mystery and a whole lot of fun.

Each story in the *Unraveling Series* will first be published as part of a Ficstitches Yarns Kit Club. So joining the Club is the only way to read the stories and get more patterns as soon as they come out.

Abbreviations and Glossary

(See Special Stitches in patterns and Tutorials for how to work uncommon stitches)

beg beginning
blo back loop only
bpdc back post double crochet
bpdc2tog back post double crochet 2 together
bptr back post treble crochet
ch chain
ch-sp chain space
dc double Crochet
dc4tog double crochet 4 together
4dcCL four double crochet cluster
flo front loop only
fpdc front post double crochet
fpdc2tog front post double crochet 2 together
fptr front post treble crochet
hdc half double crochet
hdc2tog half double crochet 2 together
lb-sc lower bar single crochet
lb-slst lower bar slip stitch
picot edging stitch described in pattern
prev previous
Rep repeat
reverse slip knot alternative to magic ring

RS right side
sc single crochet
sc2tog single crochet 2 together
slst or sl st slip stitch
sk skip
sp(sps) space(s)
st stitch
standing join yarn without a slip stitch in first stitch (sc, hdc, or dc)
WS wrong side
yo yarn over
[ ] Work instructions within brackets as many times as indicated
( ) Work all stitches within parenthesis into the same stitch or space as indicated; Or indicates number of stitches or repeats for an alternative size
* Repeat instructions after a single asterisk as many times as indicated
* to ** Repeat instructions between single asterisk and double asterisk as many times as indicated

Difficulty Levels

Advanced Beginner – Projects with basic stitches and simple shaping and finishing.
Intermediate - Projects using a variety of techniques, including unusual stitches.
Experienced – Projects with complex stitch patterns. In this book that is primarily cables worked onto a background of basic stitches. If you have not worked cables before, practice on Tavey's Satchel (page 14) before tackling the larger projects.

54366627R00042

Made in the USA
San Bernardino, CA
15 October 2017